Chronicles of
A Blessed Man

Paul Haber

KPI Publishing

Sale of this book without a front cover may be unauthorized. If this book is coverless, it may have been reported to the publisher as "unsold or destroyed" and neither the author nor the publisher may have received payment for it.

KPI Publishing – Trade Paperback – 2nd Edition

Copyright © 2016 by Paul Haber
Published by KPI Publishing, 2018

ISBN-13: 978-0-692-08582-0

All rights reserved. With the exception of excerpts for review or educational purposes, no part of this book may be reproduced or transmitted in any form or by any means, electronic or mechanical, including photocopying, recording, or by any information storage and retrieval system. Please purchase only authorized electronic and hardcopy editions, and do not participate in or encourage electronic piracy of copyrighted material. Your support of the author's rights is appreciated. Religiously, you'll gather brownie points for the after-life. Karma-wise, you'll lead an uneventful happy life with lots of good friends and admirers.

Printed in the United States of America

9 8 7 6 5 4 3 2

ACKNOWLEDGEMENTS

First, as I prepare to publish a Second Edition of this story, I thank God, my Father in Heaven, for giving me the opportunity to write this, and a couple more books that are on the way.

I thank my new friend, D'Norgia Taylor-Price, for the advice, help and mentorship required to get this job done. You are a God-send.

I also thank J Carrell Jones, author of Enemy Me and GRID Traveler Trinity, for helping me through some troublesome publishing landmines.

Lastly, I thank Kyehwa, my long-suffering spouse, both for putting up with me all these years- it's been forty, now- and for always "having my back" in whatever I tried to do. I love you, Babe!

David –
The best
son-in-law ever

Paul Kahn

Paul Haber

Chronicles of A Blessed Man

Paul Haber

Chronicles of A Blessed Man

CHAPTER 1
MAN DOWN

You've heard of déjà vu? Much of what I experienced while in the coma seemed to be happening for the second or third time, but I "knew" it was the first. Confused? Me too!

I was in a huge field, a barren, nasty place with big rocks and flames shooting up from the ground in random patterns of blue, red, and orange. Out of the flames came all sorts of creeps, ghouls, dragons, -and most frighteningly, -devils with horns and all. All of them had drawn a bead on me and were coming to get me with intentions I didn't even want to guess.

I was running through the rocks, leaping and trying to dodge the flames while trying to elude the "nasties." That was bad enough, but the scene kept replaying. I knew it was replaying but couldn't seem to get past it. Remember the movie, Ground Hog Day? It was kind of like that but combined with Rosemary's Baby. I knew I had been here before but couldn't change it. I couldn't "get off the ride."

When I was a child, I frequently had dreams where I was being chased usually by a dark, frightening monster of some kind. I'm told it's quite common among children. I don't know how common it is, but it was for me. But those dreams were never this bad or this intense, and I hadn't experienced that type of dream for many years. In these dreams, I could feel the heat of the flames and smell the sulfur belching up from the crevices in the rock. The demons were real- to me at least. They had substance, and the dragons and other strange beasts had a strength and texture I've never experienced in a dream before.

Meanwhile, from somewhere far away, I heard my wife Kyehwa's voice saying, "Come on, Ranger. You've been through Hell before. You can make it through this. You're a Ranger. You're tough." Sometime later, I thought I heard her say, "Not yet. You've made too much mess. You have to clean up. You can't go yet."

I wasn't sure that was her. Maybe it was my guardian angel. Keep in mind that this was during the time I was in an induced coma. I found out some time later that some of this actually happened, and it was the night after the first surgery on Wednesday when, supposedly, I was

Chronicles of A Blessed Man

all but gone. I never believed that a person could hear when he was "out of it," but what do I know? Only God knows how long the dreams persisted, but it must have been several days.

The dreams continued, and so did Kyehwa's voice that was telling me that if I didn't move my foot or whatever the reaction was that she wanted, she would "pinch my nipple." She says I tried to grin even through the oxygen mask. I felt something gently scratching my head, my back, and my arms. But it seemed very far away—and it was mixed in with the nightmares, all very confusing, and really not worth the effort. I was too busy dodging the monsters!

I didn't remember it at the time, but all this started several hours, or maybe days, earlier…

The pain! My gut felt as if I had been slashed with a dull sword. I fell to the floor, curled up in a ball, and screamed! I heard my wife and daughter run into the room- after that, everything kept flashing from pain to black.

It's been several years now since I came as close to death as anybody could come. Somewhere along the way to recovery while I was still in the hospital, I came up with the idea that it would be a good idea to put all this on paper—if only to allow me to get it all straight in my own head. Just for fun, let's blame my sister, Sue, who brought a laptop to the hospital and one of our friends who said it would make a good story. Okay, you asked for it!

I should tell you that after waking up in ICU at St. Joseph's Hospital, I didn't remember a single thing about what happened days previously. In fact, when Kyehwa, my long-suffering wife, tried to explain what had happened, she began with, "You had surgery…" I couldn't remember having any such plan. Total confusion!

It was only two weeks later as we sat quietly at home that she started at the beginning. I even remembered what happened prior to my collapse. Now, it seems like a distant memory, so keep that in mind as we go through this together. I hope it's interesting, maybe a little amusing, as some of it is to me. And for those who lived through it with me, I hope you'll get an idea of how much I appreciate you.

CHAPTER 2
THE DUDE

I first saw the light of day at 8:45 am on January 23, 1946. It was in a small hospital in an equally small town called Toledo, Oregon. Since we left when I was eighteen months old, I don't remember it at all. So, returning there is one of the items on my "bucket list."

My parents had met while both were serving in the U.S. Army during World War II. My mom was a photographer and sometimes secretary, and my father's occupation was sort of cloudy. Mom thought he was in Infantry, but I recently found out that he retired as a Lieutenant Colonel in the Military Intelligence with a chest full of medals to attest to his service. I guess he kept his real job secret even from his wife. It was an interesting discovery for me for reasons I'll discuss later.

Of course, in those days, a woman couldn't serve in the military if she had children or were pregnant. So, Mom, Virginia Rose Cotton nee Kelley, was discharged early. Her contract was "duration plus six months," but I changed all that. My father, Wesley Kermit Cotton, was always called Tex by Mom because he was born in Texas. He was discharged soon after and took his new wife and soon-to-be son to a logging camp in Oregon where he had been offered a job.

As I learned more about him, I found a lot of similarities between us like the propensity to take macho jobs such as lumberjack, construction, and similar fields. Nature or nurture? You decide.

They named me Wesley Paul Cotton, but since there were several other Wesleys in our family, I was Paul from the beginning. It was not Paulie or any other diminutive except for one aunt who got away with calling me "Pollywog." I really thought Aunt Hilda was special.

Two strong and headstrong people living together can be a problem. Mom was a coal miner's daughter with four older brothers. All her life, she fought for independence. In fact, she usually had a chip on her shoulder, which never changed.

I never knew my father, but he couldn't have accomplished what he did in his life unless he was pretty tough too. According to Mom, he once slapped her during an argument, and she countered by cracking him

Chronicles of A Blessed Man

across the face with a hot iron. I was never sure of that story until I found an unknown half-brother, Richard, and his family recently. He said that our father told the same story and had the scar on his forehead to prove it. Not long after that incident, he struck her again or threatened her, depending on the source of the story. When he left for work, Mom packed up, and we left.

She was never clear on how, but we made it from Toledo to Corvallis where we caught a Greyhound bus for the trek back to the sanctuary of my Aunt Harriet's house. She was my mother's elder sister and was known as Peg. She lived in the steel city of Weirton, West Virginia, so we were on the bus for almost three thousand miles. That was some thirty-nine-hour drive if you didn't stop; I never asked how many days it took on the bus, but it must've been miserable, traveling with a toddler, especially with one prone to colic.

Of course, I remember none of that as my first set of memories is of a huge, two-story house with a basement near the town of Library in southwestern Pennsylvania. We were living with Mom's parents on one side of the house, and life was great for me!

Grandpap Daniel Funk Kelley was a strict, tough, opinionated, and perhaps bigoted individual who had been a coal miner and then a steel worker. I never did get the straight explanation of why he made that change, but according to Mom and several aunts and uncles, he had been a foreman, and rather than taking the side of the company in a dispute, he fought for the union. "A troublemaker" is how one uncle described him.

He was a crotchety old guy except around me and my cousin Bobby, who lived nearby. We—especially I—got spoiled rotten! One of my favorite stories occurred when I was about three- Grandpap told Mom that he was going to buy me a suit. Mom, of course, was overjoyed until the suit turned out to be a Pittsburg Pirates baseball uniform. In most pictures around that time, I was wearing that uniform usually with cowboy boots, and often with cowboy guns strapped to my waist, as well.

Grandpap would play ball with me for hours, catching my hardest throws or increasingly sharp hits with a bat, bare-handed. Years later, arthritis had taken over his hands, and they became permanently cupped. Some of our relatives told me that it was because of all the hard catches while playing ball with me. He seldom missed a Pirates' game on the radio; he would sit next to the old Zenith radio, leaning very closely to the speaker due to a combination of tinny output and bad hearing. I recall he even took me to one game in Pittsburg where I watched my hero, Ralph Kiner, put one over the left

Chronicles of A Blessed Man

field fence. I love baseball to this day. Ralph Kiner hit 369 home runs, had a lifetime batting average of .279, and was admitted to the Baseball Hall of Fame in 1975 for those of you are fans.

I remember the Christmas before my fifth birthday. Grandpap and my uncles teamed up and got me two pairs of boxing gloves and an honest-to-goodness punching bag, a speed bag, which soon was hung in the "coal house" behind our home. It was a great Christmas for a while. I was pounding away at my uncles, who let me get away with it. Then Mom decided that if I were going to hit, I needed to feel what the other guy felt. She put on the gloves, got down on her knees, and pop! My first black eye. I don't really remember the aftermath, but Mom said everybody got on her case really badly. That was the beginning of my boxing career, which continued through the Golden Gloves and boxing in the Third Marine Division.

I think it was the following summer, and I was riding my tricycle on the hilly lawn outside Grandma's house, which she rented half of from Hazel and Jack Harrison. I lost control and flew down a long flight of stone steps, ending up in the "red-dog" gravel road below. I got six stitches on my lip, but I was lucky that I wasn't killed.

Paul Haber

The stitches were painful, but the ice cream afterward was wonderful. It was my reward for being brave.

But they say only Heaven lasts forever, and sometime around late 1951, Mom met a guy. I think Peter Haber was originally dating Mom's girlfriend, but that didn't last too long. Anyway, that's when the trouble started. Pete was a soldier, and that was all right. But—gasp—he was Polish…and a Catholic. Grandpap told Mom, in no uncertain terms, that she wouldn't go out with "that Hunkie" if she wanted to live in his house. We moved out a few days later.

Mom turned to Janie McKenna, a friend who convinced her parents to take us in. Jim McKenna was an Allegheny County Police Officer, a county cop as we called him. Jim and his wife Rachael, Rae, lived in a huge home provided by the county. He needed it for his large family and us. It was a beautiful place on the side of a hill, white, with porches on both levels that almost wrapped around all the way. It was a true mansion with manicured lawns on all sides, and a long, winding driveway leading to Highway 88. Years later, the county turned it into a ski resort.

We stayed there almost a year, and two things spring to mind about that period. First, Rae McKenna made it clear to my mom that we were going to attend church—

Chronicles of A Blessed Man

either the Catholic Church the McKennas attended or another of Mom's choice. But we would attend somewhere. Prior to that, we had infrequently attended, I think, a Southern Baptist Church near my grandparent's home, which happened to be on...yep, you guessed it. Church Hill Road. Mom felt very uncomfortable there. She felt the other women looked down on her because she was a "Grass Widow," a divorcée. According to her, wives would hold on to their husbands' arms when she walked down the aisle. I was too young to notice, but I always wondered... Mom was pretty but not that exceptional.

Anyway, we started going to St. Valentine's Catholic Church, and something about it appealed to me. Maybe it was the music or the liturgy. I don't really know. It wasn't much later that I told mom I wanted to become a Catholic at the age of six. To say she was surprised was an understatement; shock would probably be a better word. The other exceptional memory from that year was my exposure to Pee Wee football. The McKennas' son, Jim Junior, coached a team, and they practiced in the field adjacent to the house. I loved watching them practice. Those kids looked gigantic; they were really grown up- like twelve years old.

Paul Haber

In June of 1952, Mom and Pete were married, which was almost two weeks to the day after she told him she wouldn't marry him if were "the last man on earth." It was a small event with Janie McKenna and her boyfriend Wade as the only witnesses. I found out about it two days later. Shortly after, Pete, now Dad, was discharged, and he bought a brand new 1952 Chevrolet pickup truck. We moved to his home town, Lockport, New York. At that time, Lockport was the home of the Tuco Jigsaw puzzle factory and two separate General Motors plants. The Main Plant was near downtown and only a block from the house we lived in for several years. The West Plant was on the far side of the town. It was a relatively small city but managed to have most of the amenities—good and bad—a larger city would have like parks, parades, traffic jams, and the 50's version of street gangs, which I managed to become involved in later.

One of the first things I realized was that my days of being spoiled were over. This was a brand new world! I was expected to do more and more work each year. Playtime was optional, and discipline was strict. At about the age of twelve, I was spending my summer cutting grass on about an acre of orchard and yard, working in a large garden on the" farm" we had moved

Chronicles of A Blessed Man

to, and caring for several goats. It also included milking twice a day and feeding chickens and ducks. There were also two sisters and a brother to babysit for no pay. We were not given an allowance. It was my dad's famous line that he wanted us "to be good for nothing." I got the humor many years later.

My dad's philosophy about raising children was just about the direct opposite of mine. He believed a kid should be kept busy to keep out of trouble; I wanted to play and explore the fields and woods in the area. Recently, someone asked me about the happiest memory of my childhood. I didn't even have to think about it. It was me running free through the fields with no one to tell me to stop. It usually only happened when Dad was at work.

We fought constantly, usually verbally, but sometimes physically. He was tough. Today, we would call his methods abusive. We never really had a good relationship until a few years before he died when I was in my fifties.

When I turned seventeen, I escaped to the U.S. Marine Corps. Talk about going out of the frying pan into the fire. However, I put in four years, made Sergeant in three, and survived an extended tour in Vietnam before taking a discharge. Looking back, I see that Dad managed, somehow, to teach me work ethic and accountability, which helped me in the Corps and since.

I swore I would never wear a uniform again—no Fire Department, no Police, and definitely no military! For the next seven years, I was a civilian and an unhappy camper. I married shortly after returning home to a girl I had only actually been with a total of twenty-eight days before we tied the knot.

To make it plain, Sue and I made each other miserable. Basically, I married her because she was available and because her father told us we couldn't. She married me because I was the first guy she had met who would tell her father where to go; not a good start to a happy marriage. We would fight on almost a daily basis, then we would make up only to fight again the next day. I have to take a lot of the blame for that. I was very selfish and cared not at all about her feelings. On the other hand, Sue never learned that lying and writing bad checks were not a good idea. It's a wonder our marriage lasted as long as it did.

In 1973, I gave up on civilian life and went back to where I finally realized I belonged. The Army offered me what the Marines couldn't—a career in Special Operations. So, I became a soldier. All during my childhood, I had talked about being a soldier, a Marine,

Chronicles of A Blessed Man

or some sort of warrior for the United States. After the four years in the Corps, I thought I had had enough. Wrong! It took me seven years, seventeen jobs, thirteen addresses, four and a half kids, and hundreds of sleepless nights to realize I belonged in uniform. Returning was one of the smartest moves I ever made on a lot of levels.

I served three years in the Infantry, was accepted to Special Forces, passed the Special Forces Qualification Course, and the Army Ranger School at age thirty-four (ten years older than most of my classmates). I learned to skydive, swim long distances in the open ocean, climb mountains, blow things up with home-made explosives, and shoot pretty much every kind of rifle and pistol. Fun stuff! I was chosen for several "Gray" and" Black" Operations, and finally, a classified, plain-clothed assignment with Military Intelligence in Korea. I had a fine time until I realized in my forties that it was getting harder to recover from the injuries and general wear and tear of my profession. It was time to retire. Kyehwa and I had decided to move back to Tucson to be near my Mom, who was getting on in years. There, we stayed for more than two decades.

I worked fifteen years for the Arizona Department of Corrections as an Officer, Sergeant and counselor, had recently retired when the pain hit, and my life changed.

Paul Haber

Actually, I'm twice retired—the first from the U.S. Army Rangers and Special Forces as I mentioned and the second from Arizona Department of Corrections. I keep myself in pretty good shape. In fact, despite my being in seventies now, people say I'm some kind of a workout freak! I teach Karate and Jujutsu a few times a week, do an exercise program called CrossFit, and just generally try to act like a kid half my age. It hurts sometimes, but it's worth it! I guess I'm not the type to sit around and watch TV. I also operate a web-based business, which brings in some money and it also allows me to help others duplicate what I do in a type of mentorship program.

Although I had grown older and matured somewhat over the years, I was still certainly not what you would call a "people person," which is strange since my business and my martial arts required me to deal with people regularly in a positive manner. That could be why I lost many students, and the business was only marginally profitable.

Often, when I was an officer in the Army, my supervisors would make jokes like, "Haber thinks tact is spelled t-a-c-k!" I was many times counseled about my rudeness and my short temper. Most of my leadership

Chronicles of A Blessed Man

consisted of giving orders then shouting when they weren't followed quite the way I expected.

On top of all that, I bought into the "Macho" image that said it was all right to fool around even though I was married to one of the finest women on earth.

One of my kids coined the term, "obstreperous, recalcitrant, curmudgeon," an uncontrollably noisy, uncooperative, stubborn old killjoy. That about summed it up!

I will give you a telling example. Someone gave my wife, Kyehwa, a picture of several of our grandchildren with a frame that said, "Grandma's House. Kids spoiled here."

Very cute, but one of my granddaughters commented, "Unless Dude is home!" The kids called me Dude.

On August 24, I was scheduled to drive to Ontario, California, to hear a business coach of mine speak. As I look back, I think the real reason I wanted to drive so far was to impress upon Brad that I was serious and deserved his attention and mentorship help. That was probably not the best reason, but it was mine.

However, Someone Else had other ideas. Both cars broke down within two days of each other—nothing major but enough to make it impossible for Kyehwa and me to make the trip. It was really dumb stuff, a leaking plastic coolant reservoir in one vehicle and a broken exhaust pipe bracket in the other. Unbelievably to me, at the time, parts were not locally available and would take several days to arrive.

If I had gone to California, I would've been somewhere in the desert west of Phoenix, Arizona when I became seriously ill. Coincidence? I don't think so, but you make up your own mind. I believe I was being protected from my own stupidity.

In fact, Linda Cornett, one of our neighbors and very close friend, reports that on the morning of the 24th, I made the statement that, "Someone's trying to tell me not to go."

I started the day as usual with coffee and a "gut-buster" workout. This one consisting of walking lunges 400 meters up and down hill in the hundred-plus degree heat followed by a breakfast of rice eaten as cereal with milk, which, God bless her, Kyehwa can never understand. She's Korean and just can't fathom why anyone would ruin a good bowl of rice with milk! The rice was kind of dry, and I was wondering why anyone would ruin a good bowl of milk with rice! To this day, we disagree about that rice. I remember a dish of cold rice, kind of dry. She says it was a fresh pot she had just cooked that morning. Now, I ask you, friend, who are

Chronicles of A Blessed Man

you gonna believe, Kyehwa or the guy who came out of the coma? Never mind.

Since I was retired, my days were actually more filled with activity than when I had a job. Between working out, running errands, and some reading, the days seemed to slip by. I'm also a sun-freak, so any chance to get out was a good excuse and usually not a problem in Southeastern Arizona. This is true especially in August when the temperature easily gets to one hundred and ten every day just before the monsoon rain hits in the mid-afternoon and turns everything into a tropic-like flood plain with ninety-five percent humidity. Any spare time I had, I would spend with Marina's kids who had given me the nickname "Dude" after we watched Finding Nemo a few too many times.

But I also knew the sun would burn my hide and wear me out if I didn't protect myself. So, after breakfast, I climbed into a pair of jeans, boots, and a long-sleeved shirt and went into the walk-in closet to decide which hat to wear. I was trying to decide between the straw cowboy hat, which did a better job of keeping the sun off my face or the khaki "boonie hat" with its floppy brim and chin strap that was less likely to fly off in the wind. Just about then, my daughter, Marina,

Paul Haber

arrived to take us to her house where I had promised to cut the grass since I couldn't go to California, anyway.

CHAPTER 3
MARINA, LIKE THE BOAT DOCK

"What are you doing this evening?" the doctor asked after he had completed his examination that sunny April afternoon in 1981. We were stationed in Massachusetts, and I had taken the afternoon off to accompany my wife to the OB/GYN.

"I have night duty at my Battalion. Why?" I responded.

"Get someone else to take your duty. Your wife's going into the hospital now. She's dilated three centimeters."

I wasn't sure what that meant, but his serious tone got through to me. I made the call quickly.

Kyehwa and I had been married about three years, and she had miscarried our first child about a year before. She almost desperately wanted to have a child, but the first pregnancy had been a disaster. Right from the beginning, she had terrible nightmares, phantom pains, and depression. She dreamed of devils coming to take her baby and horrible, bloody dreams of the baby being attacked by monsters too horrible to describe. Almost every night, I would wake to hear her moaning in her sleep, frequently crying, and even screaming out loud in her sleep. I would wake her as gently as possible and hold her, but nothing seemed to help.

It was at this point I taught her to pray. She had been raised in a culture which combined Shamanism, Confucianism, and Buddhism—everything except Christianity and knew nothing about asking for help from a Supreme Being. I had been raised in the Catholic Church but had not been very active in the past few years. One part of my upbringing remained. I prayed frequently, especially in times of trouble or fear. This qualified.

I explained to her about a God who loved her, cared about her well-being, and would, if she would just ask, give her the strength to carry on even in the worst of times. I explained how I had gained strength and courage from prayer when I had been close to death in Vietnam and a few other more recent places. I taught her to think of the Lord as a loving Father, who she could go to with her needs. When she miscarried in the fifth month, it was, although tragic at the time, almost a relief. As soon

Chronicles of A Blessed Man

as she recovered, we resumed our attempts to have a baby together but were disappointed for months. It got to the point where I began to believe that I had somehow become sterile after fathering five kids previously. She began to pray with fervor, "If you give me a child, it will be your child. I will do my best to raise it well."

It was not until Kyehwa took a trip to Korea to visit her ailing mother that she realized she was pregnant. In fact, when she arrived at her mother's home, she was still oblivious until her mother informed her she was going to have a baby. She didn't believe it at first, but with her mother's help, finally put the clues together. She felt so completely different than the first time that she didn't realize she was almost six weeks pregnant. She didn't tell me until she returned and had it verified by our doctor. Joy filled our home!

I had been around pregnant women a lot in the past. I was quite a few years older than my siblings and had fathered five children with my ex-wife, Sue. I thought I was an expert. But this was different.

When the cravings started, her whole diet changed. Instead of her favored Korean cuisine, she needed pizza from a particular store, which happened to be in Tucson, several hundred miles away, or she needed ice cream in the middle of the night with the nearest open store more than ten miles away. Military bases hadn't caught on to twenty-four-hour service yet; we both lost a lot of sleep.

Under doctor's orders, I called my unit, spoke to the Sergeant Major, and told him what was happening. Without hesitation, he told me to "Take care of your bride" and not to sweat the duty.

We spent a long night as the dilation continued, but the baby hadn't descended. In fact, she was sideways in Kyehwa's womb; no way was she going into the birth canal.

Marina Lee Haber was born on April 30, 1981, by Cesarean section. I was allowed to be in the OR, which was a radical change from the medical attitudes with my five previous children. Back in the day, the father was relegated to the waiting room, not included in the process.

I got to hold Marina first when she hadn't been cleaned completely and still had flecks of blood on her. I marveled at how beautiful she was. Normally, I thought most babies, even mine, looked pretty much alike but not this one. Her skin was a gorgeous golden color, a legacy from her Korean mother, and her tiny features were a combination of Asian and western—a wonderful combination.

Chronicles of A Blessed Man

Since that happened to be one short period of my Special Forces career that I was not deployed somewhere, I got to take some leave when Kyehwa and the baby came home. After the surgery, with the attendant pain and difficulty moving around, we quickly devised a system for nighttime feeding. When Kyehwa heard the baby cry, she would nudge me. Then I would get up, bring the baby to her, and go downstairs to heat up a bottle.

By the time I returned with the bottle, Kyehwa would have already changed Marina's diaper and would feed her while I slept. Thanks to the Army, I could drop off to sleep in an instant. Once the feeding and burping were completed, I would return the baby to her bedroom, go downstairs and rinse out the bottle, and go back to bed for a couple of hours until we did it again- a great system.

Marina was actually named after the Little Mermaid in the original Hans Christian Andersen fairy tale; Disney, for some reason, found it necessary to change her name to Ariel. The baby's middle name, Lee, was an Americanization of Yi, which was Kyehwa's family name and the royal family of the Kingdom of Korea for five hundred years until 1910 when the Japanese invaded and deposed the king. No wonder Marina looked like a Princess.

Her name was prophetic even as a baby, and she loved the water. She learned to swim almost as soon as she learned to walk. Fear of the water never seemed to enter her mind. Even as a pre-teen, she would swim lap after lap in our backyard pool. When a friend of mine put a scuba tank on her back, she didn't surface until she had sucked the tank dry.

About this time, shortly after we has returned from Korea, she came up with a line that would become her trademark for years. Since we lived in Tucson, home of a great many Hispanic folks, and many people pronounced her name in the Spanish way with the rolling "R"- Mar-rina. My young daughter would promptly correct them, "My name is Marina like the boat dock!" Never was this girl shy!

She went through all the normal little-girl and teenage stuff. Her situation wasn't helped by being number six in the food chain after we had obtained custody of my other kids. She was only six months old when the older five came to live with us, so she got a little spoiled—at least until the novelty wore off, then she was subject to the usual sibling hassles.

Chronicles of A Blessed Man

She was six when we transferred to Korea. I got to take the whole family with me. At that point, the two boys and my eldest, Ronnie, had left to live with their mother, but Marina still had three sisters at home—one younger and two several years older. Kyehwa's Korean family accepted her and all the girls as if they were long-lost children. Their cousins would argue over whose house she would stay at for a week at a time. Since none of the relatives spoke much, if any, English, Marina's Korean skills grew rapidly.

At one point, Marina and her younger sister, Melissa, stayed for about two weeks on the Yi family farm about forty miles from Seoul. I used to joke that it was so far in the "boonies" they had to pump in sunlight. Truthfully, it was a beautiful setting with a valley of rice paddies and tiny villages surrounded by tree-covered mountains that were capped every morning with beautiful while clouds. The land of the Morning Calm lived up to its name. However, the lifestyle was still old-fashioned, almost primitive without indoor plumbing. An outhouse seemed pretty scary at night to two little American girls and there was no central heat or air conditioning. When the weather was chilly, the house, which consisted of two rooms, was heated by ondohl, heating- pipes running under the floor that radiated the heat from a charcoal-fired stove in the kitchen., which was itself outdoors under a cover but with no walls.

Everyone slept on the floor atop piles of thick blankets and comforters- true togetherness. Meals were eaten on that same floor, using a low table, chopsticks, and water drawn from a hand-pump. My girls experienced life almost the way it had been in Korea a hundred years earlier. There was a radio, however, no TV, no computers, and the only books were in Hangul, the Korean language. Their cousins taught them quickly how to make their own fun that was the way children have been doing it for centuries, with games and songs that were old before their grandparents were born. Almost before we knew it, our girls could go anywhere and do almost anything in Korea. They were obviously part Caucasian, but their skills, manners, and conversation were the same as any kid in that part of the world. Old ladies loved them.

It was during this period that Kyehwa enrolled Marina in a Taekwondo class. The instructor was very traditional, and everybody was treated the same, no matter what color their skin was. Marina learned the songs, the slogans, and experienced the traditional discipline along with a dozen other kids and was awarded her black belt, technically a junior black belt

Chronicles of A Blessed Man

because of her age of eight. I was able to accompany her for her test at the Kukiwon, the World Headquarters, and was pleased to see that her requirements were the same as those for adult candidates—the same techniques, the same forms, even fighting. Of course, her opponents were about her age, but it was impressive nonetheless.

Shortly after that, Marina's martial arts education continued under her sister, Alicia, with my supervision. Over the next few years, she became quite good. She even auditioned for a martial arts film and starred in several demonstrations. When she was about twelve, she had a demonstration routine in which a teen-aged boy would swing at her head with an aluminum baseball bat, and to the shock of the spectators, she would slip inside the strike, grab the bat, and use it to throw the boy several feet across the mat. She ended up with the bat and would chase him out of the crowd while everyone laughed.

Her skills in the water allowed her to become a lifeguard in addition to practicing the martial arts and frequently making the honor roll in school. She even got a series of jobs while in high school, working in dress shops and restaurants to pay her own tuition the last two years in Salpointe, a Catholic High School in Tucson.

Paul Haber

Several years before my collapse, following an unwise and doomed relationship that had netted her a beautiful son and daughter, I had introduced Marina to a martial arts associate of mine named David Chait. They had been around each other a few times at martial arts functions, and Marina had been impressed with the way David had calmed down her baby daughter at one promotion ceremony. They had never spent time together, until David came to a party celebrating my fortieth year in the martial arts and my sixtieth birthday. They had talked for a long, long time, and the rest was history. I gained a terrific son-in-law, and Marina became mother to David's three kids from his previous marriage. The way had been rocky like any new marriage, but they were working their way through it. David was also building a strong marketing business in addition to working for the government.

Marina and her husband David had about two and a half acres of property in a town called Sierra Vista, down near the border with Mexico. David worked full time doing mysterious things with computers for the Army, and Marina had several part-time jobs in addition to caring for their five children and for David's aged mom, Alice. The grass was getting out of control. I had volunteered to come down and cut the grass, or at least,

Chronicles of A Blessed Man

begin the job. I had suggested grazing some goats or cattle on it, so they tried the goats. It didn't work out as a long-term solution, and they accepted my offer to mow the stuff; today was the day.

Suddenly, as I was gathering my equipment for that job, I was hit with a terrible cramp in my abdomen. At first, I thought it was because I had eaten breakfast too fast or the rice had been too dry or…

I attempted the "fingers down the throat" routine with no result. The pain got worse. I was curled up on the floor of my bedroom moaning and finally told Kyehwa she had to take me to the Emergency Room at Benson Hospital. Somehow, the two of them got me into a car, and we started off.

To be honest, even now, I don't remember much about the trip to the hospital. I only recall asking Marina why she was "taking the long way" down the Interstate instead of the shorter way, which had more turns. She says she answered me, but I was out of it.

I recall sometime later, kneeling on a bed somewhere in Benson Hospital with my head on some sort of table or dresser, trying to make the pain go away. Curling up in a ball was the only thing I could still do.

Kyehwa tells me that the medical personnel gave me a shot for pain. Okay, if you say so!

Paul Haber

Then, a minute later, from my viewpoint, I woke up in ICU. And it was really about six days later. In the meantime, I had been transported, after a seven-hour delay, by ambulance to St. Joseph's Hospital in Tucson. They had run some tests and determined that surgery was necessary STAT- so much so that the surgeon and Kyehwa didn't wait for the hospital transportation people. The two of them shoved my gurney into the O.R. themselves. Kyehwa was then escorted to a waiting room and was told they would keep her posted.

I went into surgery on Wednesday afternoon. When they opened me up, the doctors found a portion of my small intestine that was perforated, herniated, and basically dead. When they had completed removing that part, which was about two feet, they found that the next segment was too weak to be attached, so they left me open for another two days, giving my body a chance to heal a little.

I was on total life support during this period, and Kyehwa and Doctor Harmon, the surgeon, both tell me that I was in an induced coma. I'm also told I died somewhere along the way. Thanks to modern medicine, I made it back.

Chronicles of A Blessed Man

All I know is that as I was coming out of the drugs later, I had some of the most horrific nightmares I have ever experienced. Let's talk about that in a while.

Most of what happened next was a mixture of drug-induced nightmares and what I thought were figments of my imagination. Now, I'm not so sure.

CHAPTER 4
RETROSPECT

Quite a bit was happening while I was "blissfully" sleeping in the OR and ICU. With the help of some of the participants, I'll try to tell that part of the tale. Of course, except for a few items that came through the fog, I remember nothing about this at all. If everything I have been told is true, I'm glad I don't remember!

After I passed out on Tuesday and before I woke up the following Monday, I was transported to St. Joseph's Hospital, tested, X-rayed, prodded, poked, and examined in every manner imaginable.

Kyehwa tells me that after she helped wheel me to X-ray, I cooled my heels in the hallway for a couple of hours. The staff asked me to stand to have an X-ray taken, and I was unable to stand. Of course, they handled the situation, and I was once again placed on the gurney, waiting to be transported back to my room.

Chronicles of A Blessed Man

Suddenly, my surgeon, Dr. Harmon, came "jogging" down the hall with a sheaf of papers, grabbed one end of the gurney-with Kyehwa assisting, and hurried off toward the operating room. I guess I was still conscious and wise-cracking (you would expect less?) right up until the last minute. The anesthesiologist came to talk to me.

"Oh, you're the gas guy?" I cracked.

He smiled and replied, "Yeah, I've been called that." He proceeded to explain what he was going to do…I guess.

Soon after, Kyehwa, who had been with me up until then, was shown to the waiting room and someone turned out my lights.

I went into surgery at about 2:30 pm. Shortly after 5:00 pm, Dr. Harmon entered the waiting room, looking worried and quite subdued. Things were not looking so well.

"He's a very sick man," he told Kyehwa.

She stared at him, stunned.

The surgeon continued, "What happened is a hernia in the small intestine. Part of the intestine is dead and we had to cut that off. In order to attach the parts together, the intestine has to be healthy. We tried that, but that part of the small intestine isn't strong enough to hold, so we have to stabilize him until it gets stronger."

"What gets stronger?"

Harmon again explained the problem, what he had done, and told her they would wait a day or two to allow the intestine to gain strength before again attempting to attach the two parts. "Remember," he said, "He's a very sick man."

"He's okay?" Kyehwa asked, shaking.

"Well, he has to stabilize."

"Can I go see him?"

Harmon thought for a moment, "Give him about forty-five minutes. He's in ICU Room 2 West. I'll tell the nurse to call you." As he turned to leave, he said, "Remember, he's a very sick man."

Kyehwa sat alone in the waiting room for about an hour, imagining all the worst possible things that could be happening. Finally, the nurse called and told her she could look in on me. She ran to my room, and in her words, "My heart dropped."

Not only had the medical staff inserted a gastro-nasal bypass tube in my nose, but there was an oxygen tube running from the right corner of my mouth down my throat. And some sort of plastic frame was holding my

Chronicles of A Blessed Man

face, apparently to keep the mouth open and still. She thought I looked like a corpse.

Kyehwa rubbed my arm and scratched my head—anything to make contact. She turned to the nurse, "Can I talk to him? Can he hear me?"

"You can try," the nurse told her kindly, "Some say they can hear."

My wife did her best, talking and babbling, anything she could think of to get a reaction with no visible result. The strange thing is, I know now that some of the "hallucinations" I experienced of having the same conversation many times actually happened while I was in a coma. For example, I vividly remember an "angel" saying, "You can't give up yet. You've got too much mess to clean up. You have lots more work to do." The voice, I now realize, was that of my own guardian angel, Kyehwa.

At about 7:30 PM, she finally gave up, kissed me goodbye, and started for home.

Driving by herself, Kyehwa was in turmoil. Her husband had gone into the Operating Room alive and came out dead, or so she thought. Apparently, sometime during the surgery, I had "flat-lined," and they brought me back. She was shaking so badly that she could hardly keep the steering wheel straight. What would she do if Paul died?

She saw she had a phone message from my daughter, Cori, wanting to know what was going on. Kyehwa didn't return the call because she was afraid she'd break down if she talked to any of my kids.

Suddenly, as she approached Interstate 10, she pulled to the side of the street, hands locked to the steering wheel, and just wept. Then she looked upward and prayed, "God, I don't know what to do. In fact, I don't think I can do anything. There's nothing I can do. Only You can do something."

"I'm going to give everything to you," she continued, "My heart is aching. I want you to take all my burdens and don't let me take them back. You're the only one who can cure this. So, God, help me. Whatever is, it is. Whatever you decide, it's your decision. I'm going to leave it to you. If he's gone, that's Your will. If he's alive, that's Your will. Holy Mary, I need your comfort. Tell me it's going to be okay."

"From that moment on," she told me much later, "I was fine. My heart wasn't aching. My crying stopped. I started thinking clearly, so I could drive home."

When she finally arrived at our home some forty minutes later, she began making calls to our friends,

Chronicles of A Blessed Man

Sandra Perfetto and Mike Reynolds, as well as my children to tell them what was happening.

From there, the word spread like wildfire.

After only a brief night's sleep, Kyehwa was up & at'em again. There were bills to be paid, and the deposits had been sent to the bank account, but payments needed to be sent to the creditors. She wanted to get back to the hospital.

Linda Cornett, our neighbor and friend, insisted on going with her. She had found out that Kyehwa hadn't eaten all day Wednesday and made it her business to see that she didn't starve again. There was also the matter of picking up one of our vehicles from the repair shop. Thank you, Linda!

When they arrived at St. Joseph's Hospital, Kyehwa resumed her attempts to make contact, rubbing, scratching, and so on. She even tickled my feet with no response. When she discovered my feet were cold, she turned to the nurse on duty.

"His feet are cold. Can I put socks on him?" she asked.

"If you want to put socks on him, you can," she replied.

Paul Haber

As she pulled a pair of bright yellow socks with a smiley face on each side onto my feet, Kyehwa asked, "One side of him is hot, one side is cold. Why is that?"

"Because he can't move around, his circulation isn't working like it's supposed to. That's why we have a machine to handle the circulation, breathing, and so on."

A little while later, one of the Med Techs entered the room and told Kyehwa that she had a telephone call. When she picked up the receiver, it was my brother, Pete, checking on my condition.

Back in the room, Linda was singing to me- gospel songs, naturally. My feet began moving back and forth sideways, which were the only response I had made so far. I contend that I was "dancing" to the music, but Linda thought I was saying "Stop, stop."

"Okay. Okay! I'll stop, okay?" she grumbled.

Truly talented folks are sensitive, I guess. Linda bought Kyehwa lunch just to make sure she had something and left for home about noon or one o'clock.

Later, when we were alone, Kyehwa scratched my scalp and rubbed my back to make contact. There was still no response.

"Since you missed the Bible study Tuesday, I'll have a Bible study with you," my bride told me. Then she asked the tech if a Bible was available.

Chronicles of A Blessed Man

The med tech smiled. "In a Catholic hospital, I think we can find a Bible, "she replied.

In just a few moments, one was brought to ICU, and Kyehwa went to work, sometimes struggling with the language in the Gideon version of the bible… For the next hour or so, Kyehwa read the scripture to me and asked questions in the way we did with our friends in our weekly Bible study. When I didn't answer, she said, "Hey, you're cheating! Any other time, you have a lot to say. Why not now?" No response.

Throughout the day, hospital staff advised her that the calls were coming in from people asking about my condition, my brother Pete, my sister Sue, and many others. They asked if we would like to set up a password to identify those to whom they could release information. Kyehwa had a better idea.

"Tell them to call Marina," she said, referring to my second-youngest daughter, who lived in the area. "She can handle the calls."

We later found that staff was confounded by all the calls they received by women claiming to be my daughters. They were much relieved when Marina told them about the size of our family.

"He's got a bunch of kids," she said, "Five daughters and two sons. A big bunch!" Marina was kept busy, receiving all the calls from family, as well as who knows how many friends. When the "word" had hit the Department of Corrections network, calls began coming in from as far away as Phoenix and Yuma from officers I had worked with years before. I guess we never realize how many people we impact just by living our lives.

Kyehwa knew we had business obligations to fulfill and decided it was her task to fulfill them. After several hours of attempting to revive me or to get me to respond, she changed clothes in a truck stop parking lot and drove over a hundred miles to Phoenix for a skin care seminar we had committed to attend. Marina helped out by picking up one of our newest associates, who lived in Sierra Vista near Marina's family, and transporting her to the truck stop to rendezvous.

After linking up with everyone, driving to Phoenix, and going in to the function, Kyehwa's cell phone announced that she had a call, but she had turned the ringer off, and she ignored it. The hospital then called Marina's phone. Marina handed it to Kyehwa, who found that it was St. Joseph's Hospital, informing her that I needed a blood transfusion, and they required her signature. After she explained that it was impossible for her to get to the hospital in less than several hours, the staff made an exception and took her verbal permission

Chronicles of A Blessed Man

in duplicate. Now, she was really shaken. What had happened? Why did I suddenly need blood? Worry filled her mind.

On the way home, after Marina had departed with our friend, Jonnie, Kyehwa once again felt overwhelmed.

"God, why are you letting me take it back? I don't want it back. It's your will, and God, on that note, he's going to have a second operation tomorrow. I think two doctors are supposed to be there. I'm not worried because Doctor Jesus is going to be there to guide these doctors operating on my husband. I know you're going to guide them well. I love you. Thank you."

Peace returned to her heart.

I don't believe that any of us at that point knew the depths of her faith in the Lord's ability to handle the situation.

CHAPTER 5
ANGEL AND BRIDE

It was 1977 when I had transferred to the Republic of Korea to an Infantry unit, A Company 1st Battalion 9th Infantry in the 2nd Infantry Division, guarding the Demilitarized Zone (DMZ).

My military career was going fine, but my personal life was in shambles. My wife of ten years, Sue, had informed me before I left that she would "probably not be here" when I returned. We had spent the last ten years making each other miserable, and an unwise marriage brought on by stubbornness and rebellion. I should've known it was only a matter of time.

I found out later that she was not exaggerating. She brought another man into our home only a few hours after I departed. She ended up marrying him later on, but that's another story.

When I was on duty, I was "Sergeant Rock," who ran his squad with an iron hand and a short temper. Any

Chronicles of A Blessed Man

violation of the rules was handled swiftly, and in most cases, illegally, with my fists. The only saving grace, I guess, was my tendency to be fair. If you obeyed the rules, I "had your back." My soldiers quickly learned this and performed for me properly and consistently. One of my goals was never to have to "write up" one of my troops for a minor infraction. I didn't want to handicap a potential future leader because he had made a youthful, dumb mistake. Instead, I took my career in my hands and handled problems unofficially. The guys actually appreciated this and reciprocated. One of the soldiers in my squad, "Haber's Gore-illas," was a kid named Dave Kelly. When he was assigned to my bunch, Dave had the reputation as a goof-off, a slacker, and a failure as a soldier. My methods worked with some of my guys to the extent that when Dave left Korea, he pinned a note to my pillow that I remember to this day…

"Sergeant Haber," the note said, "When I came to Korea, I had a family who thought I was a failure, a girlfriend I couldn't trust, and a bad attitude. Thanks to you, I'm becoming someone my family is proud of, I have a new girlfriend, and I actually got promoted to Specialist Four. Thank you for making me what I can be. Dave." I didn't always do things the Army way, but kids like Dave made the risk worthwhile.

Paul Haber

Off duty, I was a mess! If I did not "have the duty" in an evening, which only occurred quite infrequently, I was in the little village outside the gate we called Toko-ri. It was officially Tong-du-chon-up, but no one ever called it that. The little town only existed to "support" the 2nd Brigade of the 2ID.

I would hang out in the bars, chasing the "business girls" until the midnight curfew then back to the barracks to sleep and begin again the next day.

One evening, after a nasty argument with my most recent girlfriend, I went into "Rosa's Cantina," a bar and restaurant with a most unusual name for a Korean dive and a place I usually avoided. I had just finished a beer and turned around to lean on the bar when the side door opened, and a young girl peeked in.

I went on point like a bird dog!

I had never seen such a beautiful girl, with long black hair, smooth Korean skin, and a curvy body under a white top and a pair of black shorts. "What an angel," I thought. I had a new mission!

I approached and asked her to dance. She refused. She said she was looking for her girlfriend to go to a birthday party. She was obviously not interested, but I was. I followed her around for about fifteen minutes, until she finally gave in and danced with me. Then I

Chronicles of A Blessed Man

managed to wangle an invitation to her friend's party. This was starting to look like a good night.

The party was a quiet one at first with just a few Korean girls who worked at various jobs at stores in Toko-ri and a couple of soldiers, who were dating the girls. It appeared that "Miss Lee" as the girl introduced herself was the fifth wheel until I came along. Strange for such a beauty!

We enjoyed the excellent Korean food, the beer, and the Soju, a distilled Korean beverage, for about an hour until someone began pounding on the door. One of the girls opened it and found a young American soldier outside, who seemed to very angry about something. He was upset because the girl he considered his girlfriend was attending the party with another guy. Oops!

She argued for several minutes with no result, and the volume of the argument grew louder by the minute. The soldier who was with the young lady seemingly had nothing to say, and the other guy wouldn't go away.

Enough was enough!

I went to the door and confronted the youngster. He seemed to recognize me as a Sergeant in his unit. His eyes got bigger, and he backed away from the door. I found out later he was from one of the other platoons in A Company and had seen me "correcting" one of my troopers behind the barracks recently. It only took a few minutes to convince him that he was no longer needed there and that if he were really smart, he would go away. He complied, and the party went on.

After the party, I walked Miss Lee to where she told me she lived and headed back to the base, just in time for Midnight curfew. Only later, when I tried to find her again, did I discover that she had misled me about the location of her room. I guess she was trying to get rid of me. In retrospect, who could blame her?

It was several months before I found her at a party thrown by our Company Commander to celebrate successfully passing the IG Inspection. The Inspector General Inspection was an annual event in which every nut, bolt, weapon, pair of boots, and haircut was checked with a fine-tooth comb. It could be a career-killer for a commander whose unit failed, so Captain Purcell was a happy camper when we attained an almost perfect score. As Training NCO for the Company, I had major responsibility for the documentation of all the training accomplished in the past year, and I got the job a month before the inspection. I had a lot of catching up to do, fortunately, because it was about this time Sue filed for divorce back in Georgia. Captain Clifford B Purcell, who had recently gone through a divorce himself, kept

Chronicles of A Blessed Man

me working from "oh-dark –thirty" until late at night, which kept my mind off my situation, and incidentally, resulted in getting the necessary work done. I was never sure, which was Clifford B's primary objective. They called him "The Bony Ranger" due to his almost emaciated build, but he was one of the toughest men I've ever had the pleasure to work for. One of my extra jobs, when we went to the field, was to make sure that he actually at a meal once in a while since he tended to forget, in all the excitement. The company medic's job was to make sure the Captain remembered to take care of his feet.

The night of the celebration, I was circulating, enjoying the free beer and fellowship when I spotted her across the room and zeroed in! I soon found that she had been invited to the party by Joe Apodaca, our company clerk and a good friend of mine. Curses! One rule I abided by was never to interfere with another guy's girl. I talked with Joe and Miss Lee for a while and went about the serious business of partying.

It took almost six months before I finally located her again, and again, it was by accident. This time, I learned where she lived, and we began to see each other daily. I enjoyed her company, but I had no other intentions since my plan was to get back to the States, pick up a car I was ordering, and continue with my life. God had other ideas.

One night, after having dinner with Miss Lee, whose real name was Yi Kyehwa, in the Korean manner of listing last name first, I was headed back to the base in time for curfew. Curfew ran in Korea from midnight to five am, and police enforced the ban strictly. I had been telling her about my plans after I returned home, and for some reason, felt extremely depressed. As I approached the back gate to Camp Hovey, I suddenly stopped dead in my tracks. It was as if a light suddenly went on.

"Oh, no!" I thought. "It can't be! Not now!" But it was. I was in love. I had promised myself after the fiasco with Sue that I was going to remain single for a long, long time before I let myself be hurt again. But the more I thought about it, the more certain I was that this was the right move, the right girl.

I didn't sleep much that night, and my soldierly duties the next day seemed to take a month, but finally I got back into town and was knocking on her door. She let me in, and we talked awhile, but I couldn't stand the strain.

"Will you marry me?" I blurted out like a thirteen-year-old with his first love.

Chronicles of A Blessed Man

"What?" She looked at me as if I had lost my mind. Maybe I had. "No!"

"Why not? Don't you want to come to the States with me?"

"Why would I want to go to the States? I'm a Korean girl."

I didn't know quite how to answer that since every young girl I had met in Korea was on the lookout for a husband who would take her to America. And I had found the only one who wanted to stay in Korea!

That began several days of talking, convincing, and cajoling—all to no effect. I proposed five times and was turned down each time. I thought about it, I meditated, and I talked to myself. I even sat on the side of a mountain in the rain, trying to come up with some argument that would convince her I was serious. No luck.

Finally, I went back into town to a bar and ordered a magnum of Soju. At this point in my life, I seldom drank straight liquor, especially Soju, which I thought tasted like kerosene. But tonight, since it was the strongest drink available, it seemed the thing to do. About half-way through the bottle, one of my soldiers, Dave Kelley, came over to see what had upset me so greatly. I tried to explain, but the more I tried, the angrier I got. Finally, I slammed the bottle down in front of him and said, "Here, Dave, you drink this! I have something to do!"

"Sarge, wait! Where are you going?" His answer was the door closing behind me.

I went straight to Miss Lee's apartment, a small two room suite, and slammed the door open and barged in. She was lying on the bed. I realized later she had been crying, and I stormed over to her.

"Now, you listen to me!" I commanded. "I'm through playing around with you. You're going to marry me! If I can't get the paperwork done in time, you're coming to the States on a Fiancée visa. If you don't come, I'll come back and drag you by your beautiful hair. Do you understand?"

She looked up at me with her big brown eyes. "Okay!"

That began our journey together.

Kyehwa's relationship with the Lord and the Blessed Virgin had begun many years before when she was still a child. Though her parents were not Christians, one sister had gained the faith and took Kyehwa to a Catholic Church in Seoul, Korea. There, the young girl had been terrified by the strange statues and the people mumbling low as they prayed. Nothing in her life had prepared her for this. It was many years later, after we had met and

Chronicles of A Blessed Man

married, that she understood what had been happening that day.

A short time after we came to the States, Kyehwa became pregnant. It was a difficult, frightening pregnancy, especially for a girl in a strange land with no family or friends to help or console her. During that period, she told me of many terrible dreams and about a beautiful lady who gave her comfort. Although we lost the baby, Kyehwa's faith in "the lady" continued. A few years later, after seeing a statue of Mary at the Mission San Xavier de Bac in Tucson, she realized that the "lady" of her dreams was the Blessed Virgin, wearing a crown of flowers. Her faith in the Mother of Christ has continued to grow to this day. I realize that some folks don't believe that saints directly intervene in our lives, but we do. I could probably fill another book with stories but some other time!

That Friday morning, while I was unconscious and after she sent an e-mail to our youngest daughter, Melissa, filling her in on the situation Kyehwa received a call from my oldest son, Paul, in North Carolina.

"Mom, are you okay?" he asked.

"I'm fine."

Paul Haber

"Yeah, he retorted sarcastically." This is my Mom, being tough." Kyehwa has a well-deserved reputation for hiding her sadness or distress.

"No, really, PJ, I'm fine," she said. Now, the tears began welling up.

"How's Dad?"

"About the same," she answered.

"How about you?"

"I'm okay. But the doctor said he needed a blood transfusion, and I don't understand why. So, I'm on my way there now."

"Do you want me to come?"

"No," she replied. "They're supposed to have a second surgery today. Why don't you wait until after that?"

After a brief conversation in which Paul kept asking how she was doing, and she tried not to break down on the phone, Kyehwa said, "Look, I got to go!"

Again, she had to pull over and let the tears flow, and she began to pray, sobbing. "Whatever it is, is, God. It's your will, not mine. I believe in you. I believe Doctor Jesus will be there to guide the doctors. Holy Mary," she continued, "Please, just comfort me, hold me, and let me know everything will be fine." Her faith in the Lord and

Chronicles of A Blessed Man

belief in the Blessed Virgin never wavered throughout this whole crisis.

She said later that without stopping to pray, she wouldn't have been able to make the drive to the hospital.

Arrival at the hospital brought support. Friends began to arrive at St. Joseph's—first Sandra Perfetto and her son James, who bought lunch for the group, as well as ever-dependable Marina. In the afternoon, more friends, Deborah Han, my former supervisor and Jim Byrd, an old friend and martial arts student, arrived. They made sure Kyehwa had some food and got some rest—just generally were a blessing to her until the surgeons completed the second surgery, which began at 2:45 and lasted until 6:00 pm.

This time, Doctor Harmon came out of the OR with a different attitude. He was smiling! As soon as everyone saw him, they knew I was going to be okay. Harmon verified what they had suspected. I had come through the surgery in good shape and should be waking up in day or so.

There was an impromptu celebration in the ICU waiting room that afternoon, a real Hallelujah Breakdown! I'm really sorry I missed that party!

Paul Haber

After each of the visitors had a chance to see me, while I was still asleep of course, they left and Kyehwa headed for home. Marina traveled to the Tucson Airport to pick up Melissa, who had flown in from Orlando.

CHAPTER 6
PEEJAY THREE

"Mister Haber, you have a boy!"

I let out a whoop that echoed through the hospital. After three daughters, I finally had a son! Joy does not describe what I felt that day in 1973.

Sue and I were living in a village called Medina, New York, about half-way between Buffalo and Rochester, and our marriage was struggling to say the least. We would fight, then make up for a day or so only to fight again. I believe today that Sue's fears and doubts were a big factor, but my attitude didn't help either. At any rate, each time a child became a toddler, Sue would get pregnant again even though she was supposedly using several kinds of birth control.

Deliberately? I don't know, but Paul John Haber III, immediately PJ, came only fifteen months after his sister, Alicia.

Paul Haber

The stress of the hospital expenses was much less than it had been previously. I had a job with medical benefits for the first time. A couple of days after PJ was born, when Sue and the baby were released from the hospital, our first stop was the dojo- my martial arts school. It was a large room over the fire house, owned by the village, and used for my karate classes on Tuesday, Thursday, and Saturdays.

Sue said she felt well enough to climb the stairs, so I carried the baby and helped her ascend. As we reached the top, we saw a class in progress under Doug Marshall, a brown belt. When he spotted us, Doug shouted, "Mate! Stop!" He gestured toward us, and the class turned to face us.

"To the next generation, Rei!" Bow! The class honored my son and me by bowing deeply as if to a teacher. I was choked up!

PJ was my mini-me. Not only was the physical resemblance with a younger me uncanny, his attitude, likes, and dislikes were so close it was scary.

After Sue and I divorced, I missed all my children, but I had a special ache for PJ. When they finally came to live with us, PJ, however, seemed to always be in trouble just like his father had, I'm sorry to say; extremely active, aggressive, all boy.

Chronicles of A Blessed Man

But in a family of seven children, and with not enough fatherly supervision due to my military duties, those traits were causes for anger and perhaps too much discipline. Finally, after several years, PJ and his brother, Derek, went back to live with his mother, and we had virtually no contact for a while. Then, one Thanksgiving Day, when PJ was a senior in high school, he called me. What a surprise!

"Dad, I have a question. When you were young, did you ride bulls?"

"Of course, I did. I thought you knew that. Why?"

After a short pause, he answered, "I've been riding lately, and my mother says I'm just like my father. I wanted to find out if I was."

Our relationship grew swiftly over the next few years. PJ fell in love with a girl named Sammi, who gave him a son, whom he named Dakota John, before their young, immature marriage finally fell apart.

My son had enlisted in the Army for one tour then tried civilian life where he worked as a horse wrangler in a resort in Tucson, salesman for a call center, and several other things. He suffered the same boredom and discouragement I had experienced until he joined the Navy with hopes of becoming a SEAL. Unfortunately, his attempt to join their ranks was cut short when he was seriously injured during SEAL training. He went back to the fleet but hated it.

One serendipity of his short, one-tour, Navy career was meeting Christine, the love of his life, who gave him a daughter, Angelica and another son, Matthew. She raised all three kids and helped Paul- he was "too old" to be called PJ, he said- to become a good solid man. He later went back into the Army Airborne where he was still serving when he called Kyehwa to check on me, but he was simultaneously studying to become an ordained minister. He likes to stay busy.

Chronicles of A Blessed Man

CHAPTER 7
WOMEN OF POWER AND POWERFUL WOMEN

Saturday was a busy day for everyone except me. The doctor had previously told Kyehwa that I should be coming off life support on Saturday and possibly waking up on Sunday. The 'word" went out, and the daughters began to gather. Marina, of course, had been in and around ever since the Emergency Room in Benson. Melissa arrived on Friday evening, was picked up by Marina, and spent the night at our home with Kyehwa and Marina. The girls shared our queen-size bed while Kyehwa slept in the walk-in closet…by choice.

About this time, Alicia, my third daughter, arrived with her husband Travis and two of their three children, having driven some sixteen hours non-stop from Hewitt, Texas, near Waco. They slept on a queen-sized air mattress provided by Linda Cornett, our neighbor, in the living room while the children slumbered in the sewing room, another bedroom. Alicia had always been my China Doll. I remember…

"It's a boy…no, you're a girl, aren't you, baby?"

These were the first words I spoke to my third daughter that day in May, 1971. I wanted a son so badly that I almost didn't see the obvious truth.

All during that pregnancy, her mother, Sue, had expressed a desire to deliver the baby at home. According to her, the doctor had said, "You've never had any problem delivering the first two. Go ahead. If anything comes up, just call me." To my shame and embarrassment, I never followed up with a call to the OB/GYN. I just took Sue's word for it. Some people never learn.

Alicia slid out of the canal easily as I supported her head and shoulders. Her lower body flopped softly onto the stacked and folded blankets that were ready for her. I lifted her, making sure her airway was clear of blood and placenta, held her by the ankles the way I had seen done, and gave her bottom a slap.

"Heh!" More of a grumble than a cry. I tried again. Same result. I was getting a little worried about her lack of noise as her older sisters were great criers. I found Sue's compact mirror and held it near the baby's nose and mouth. I waited a few seconds and sat back with a sense of relief. She was breathing.

After I cleaned the baby, Sue, and the bed, I called the doctor to let him know we'd delivered all right. This was followed by what sounded like an explosion over the phone.

"What's the matter with you two? What do you think you're doing? Don't you know how dangerous this is? Get your wife and daughter to the hospital now!"

"But, but—'' I stammered. "You gave permission to deliver at home. I was supposed to call you if there were any problems."

"I never said any such thing," he retorted. "Get them to Medina Hospital now!"

I moved! Because the baby had been born outside the hospital, she could not be kept in the nursery, so mother and daughter took up both halves of a semi-private room designed for two patients. Of course, we had no health insurance, so it took a while to pay all those bills. Years!

Right from the beginning, Alicia Katrina looked like a porcelain or china doll or an angel on a Christmas tree. She was a little quieter than her sisters, and as our family grew, she was nicknamed "Miss Goody-goody" by her siblings. I figured out later that it wasn't that she never did anything wrong, but when she did, we didn't catch it.

Paul Haber

After Sue and I divorced, Alicia, with her sisters and brothers, came to live with my new wife and me.

Like all of our family, she was a martial artist. At one point, in Fort Devens, Massachusetts, our family would practice karate two hours a day, five days a week, any time I was at home, and most of the time if I was gone. Alicia was the first of my children to earn her black belt under me, a record she held for more than a decade before Melissa earned hers. To this day, only three daughters have attained that rank in the system I teach.

She was a good student, pretty enough to be a model, which we tried at one point in her teens with very little trouble, so she earned some trust. In her senior year in high school, as I was finishing my last year in Korea and the Army, we sent her home to live in the house we had just purchased in Tucson. She would be alone until Kyehwa, and the two younger girls joined her later. All went pretty smoothly with no wild parties or the like even though the only supervision she received was an occasional visit from my brother, Pete, who lived forty miles away. We bought her a car, so she could get around and prayed that we weren't giving her too much responsibility. She had to work to pay for her gasoline and do her own cooking and cleaning.

Chronicles of A Blessed Man

Kyehwa and the two remaining girls joined her two months later in November, and the transition went quite smoothly. Alicia went to school, found a job at a local movie theater, and continued to be a joy.

Finally, one day not long after she had graduated and I had returned home, she got very upset with me because I had criticized a house-painting project I had assigned her. When I told her, rather harshly, to "Do it again! And do it right this time," she decided enough was enough, and she moved out.

Shortly after, she married her boyfriend, Travis, put herself through the University of Arizona, received a degree in Accounting, and began to raise three kids in a relatively short time. Always a "type A" is my little girl.

Travis's career in the Air Force and beyond required them to move several times, and they finally landed in Hewitt, Texas. So, when the woman at my bedside told me she was Alicia, I knew she couldn't be. Alicia was a sixteen-hour drive away. Who was this woman, anyway?

At first, after getting back home that night, the younger girls, Marina and Melissa, argued about who would get to sleep in "Mommy's bed." Kyehwa settled the issue by giving them the bed while she slept on a yo—a futon-type mat- in the closet. She claims she slept better there than she had been in the bed.

Paul Haber

Even when I'm at home, she wakes up at any noise or movement in the house. Normally, she goes right back to sleep. When I was sick, however, she would wake up and have a lot of difficulty dropping back off. In the closet, with the door closed, in total darkness, and the mighty dog Simba (all fourteen pounds of him) at her side, Kyehwa managed to get five uninterrupted hours rest.

Saturday morning came, and the group drove in to Tucson and arrived at St. Joseph's ICU to find the television playing a gospel program. The gospel soon gave way to some sort of talk show that was "very negative" according to Kyehwa. Melissa quickly took command. No one has ever accused any of my daughters of being hesitant to take charge.

"Why are we watching this junk?" she demanded, shutting off the offending device. She then took out her iPhone and connected it with an ear-piece, which she placed in my ear and played inspirational music. After a while, she turned off the music and began to read Scripture, hoping that somehow the sacred words would penetrate the coma and help me to recover.

Although raised in the Catholic faith and attending Catholic High School, Melissa had drifted away from Christianity for several years, following the tenets of

Chronicles of A Blessed Man

Wiccan. It was only after she married her husband Kern and began associating with some of his business mentors that she returned to the Lord. She preferred a Non-denominational approach and was strong in her faith.

Since children weren't allowed in ICU, Alicia's children, Katie and Cameron, were relegated to the waiting room while the girls and Kyehwa watched me in relays. During that Saturday, Sandra Perfetto and my brother Pete also came to check on my condition. I slept on, being oblivious.

I had met Sandra Perfetto several years before. She had even been my supervisor in the Department of Corrections for a while. She, her husband Mike, and her young daughter Colleen, had become close friends. Colleen even lived with Kyehwa and me for a year while she attended the University of Arizona in Tucson. At this time, Sandra had left the Department and was living in Wilcox, Arizona. The one-and-a-half-hour drive to visit was a good example of the wonderful heart of this great friend.

Paul Haber

CHAPTER 8
THERE'S ONLY ONE SANDRA

The knock on the hallway door behind me startled me a little. I spun around in my chair outside the sally port. In the hallway stood a blonde woman in civilian clothes.

I think it was about May 1996, and I was a Corrections Officer working in the control room for the 4 C/D wing of Cimarron Unit, Arizona State Prison Complex in Tucson. The door to my control room opened into a sally port, sort of a small room that separated it from still another door. The doors opened electronically, and only one door could be opened at a time. This was to prevent any unauthorized personnel from gaining access to the control room or the "pod" as we called the cell block.

The blonde had a badge pinned to her belt, plus she obviously had access to the prison itself, so I "popped" the door and began the process of letting her in. I didn't

Chronicles of A Blessed Man

look at the badge other than to verify it was from DOC. After the hallway door was secure, I pressed the button to electronically unlock the control room door.

"Hi, I'm Sandra Perfetto," she said as she entered. "Need a floor walk?"

"Yeah, thanks," I replied and hit the buttons again to give her access to the pod. I watched as she made the rounds, going from cell to cell, looking in the small window set in each steel door, and observing what the inmates were doing in their ten-by-twelve rooms.

I assumed she was a new Corrections Officer III, a type of counselor, who was being helpful. She did a thorough job, verbally correcting some minor infractions as she progressed around the cellblock. She had obviously done this before. Some CO IIIs were hired for that position, trained in the same academy as the uniformed officers or CO IIs. Others were in uniform first then promoted into the higher rank with some becoming Sergeants after. Watching Perfetto walk the pod, I figured she had spent some time in our brown uniform.

She stayed in my pod for the next couple of hours, performing the duties of a regular CO, which gave us time to get acquainted. My first surprise was that she was a CO IV, an upper-level supervisor and one small step below a Deputy Warden. Usually, we only saw CO IVs if we happened to be in the Admin office; their job was to supervise the CO IIIs along with who-knows-what other admin functions. To have a CO IV walk the pod not just once but several times was a rare occurrence.

Since Sandra was not in my direct chain of command, that is, not a Sergeant, Lieutenant, or Captain of Corrections, it was much easier to "let my hair down" with her, and over time, she became an excellent liaison between the officers and the higher administration. We developed a close relationship over the next couple of months, and when she found out I taught karate at my home, soon enrolled her daughter, Collen Donovan, in my class.

Our friendship has remained over the years even though I was promoted to Sergeant, transferred away, and transferred back to Tucson while she had moved to Willcox, Arizona, some hour and a half away. She had transferred to the Ft. Grant Unit, which was much closer to her new home. She and her husband, Mike, would stop by our house whenever they came to Tucson, and we would drive out to their farm, a few acres outside of Willcox, whenever we had the opportunity.

Chronicles of A Blessed Man

Sandra and Mike had decided to raise a couple of goats for milk, etc., which gave me the opportunity to share what I had learned as a teenager. My family had owned a small farm, about four acres, and managed to raise several goats, two hundred or so chickens, a few ducks, and grow about an acre of vegetables. Guess who had the job of the goats and weeding the garden. You guessed it!

Anyway, it was a pleasure to teach them what I had learned, from milking the critters to building a milk stand and fencing them in to prevent them "visiting" the neighbor's gardens. I also helped them put together a geodesic dome shelter they used as a greenhouse to extend the already long growing season in Arizona. In return, every time we visited, Sandra fed us like kings. She was a fantastic cook, who loved to try new recipes. I guess we were her guinea pigs along with Mike and their daughters, Collen and Gabby.

Both Sandra and Mike were slugging out the years until they could retire and spend more time at home with their garden and their goats. At this writing, only Mike has made the move, and Sandra is now a Probation Officer. I tell her she just can't stay away from Department of Corrections. But she was there when Kyehwa and I needed her as a true friend.

Paul Haber

CHAPTER 9
IT CONTINUES

The only negative issue that day in the hospital, other than my remaining unconscious, was due to a nurse named Carla. Unlike the rest of the excellent ICU staff, Carla seemed to feel that visitors were simply a distraction and should be limited. While previously there had been no restriction on the number of visitors, Carla insisted that only two be in my room at a time.

When Kyehwa and the girls first arrived, Carla had given them a sour look.

"If you're going to come, you need to let us know," she complained. "Otherwise, it will be too crowded, and we have to work around you."

My family complied and took turns sitting by my bed and in the waiting room for the rest of the day. Finally, about five o'clock, everyone left and retreated to our home in Benson.

Paul Haber

Alicia volunteered to fix dinner, Korean food naturally, while Kyehwa and Marina cleaned up and changed clothes. Prior to becoming ill, I had booked an Opportunity Meeting for our business with Aaron Couillard, a new young man we were working with. Since I was "out of action," Kyehwa decided it was up to her to fulfill my promise.

"Our word is our bond, and we are a team," she thought. If her quarterback was out of action, she would carry the ball.

Despite her concern about her husband, fatigue from driving some eighty miles every day with little sleep, and spending all day in the hospital, she proceeded some thirty more miles to the city of Sierra Vista and presented the very first business plan she had ever done. She had watched me do it many times, of course, but this was to be her first time, and she performed brilliantly. Aaron joined our business and became as excited as could be about his future.

Marina accompanied Kyehwa to the meeting and was surprised that her mother didn't appear to be nervous at all. She couldn't realize that this was another example of Kyehwa's faith-she had given up worry to the Lord, deciding that His will be done. It calmed her and

Chronicles of A Blessed Man

allowed her to concentrate on the details of the business plan. Her strategy worked to perfection.

Exhausted, mother and daughter returned to our place for some rest. Marina's own household was on its own! She felt her mother needed her more even than her own husband and children!

An interesting side note to that evening that Kyehwa performed so brilliant. It had been raining on and off for several days as it was usual for the Monsoon season in Southeastern Arizona. However, in this instance, the dreary weather merely added to the depression until just before sundown.

Linda Cornett glanced outside toward our house across the street and saw something she had never seen before, two complete rainbows with both ends clearly visible on both. Those rainbows were directly over the Haber house. Linda took a picture, which she showed me several days later. Very unusual!

Linda and the girls called for Kyehwa, but she was not to be distracted as she was on a mission. Finally, as she prepared to leave, Linda insisted.

"Stand right there," she ordered. Kyehwa got out of the car and gazed at the scene. As Linda took her photograph of our home, which was covered by the beautiful rainbow, standing out from the dark, stormy sky.

Another neighbor, who lived in the opposite direction, saw the same sight at the same time, all over my house. It was if God were telling them it was going to be all right.

Linda Cornett was another serendipity of our moving to the small town of Benson, Arizona. We lived in a new sub-development and were the fourth family to build there. Linda and her husband Larry were the first. Linda is a self-confessed "social butterfly" who greeted each new resident with a plate of cookies and a big "welcome to the neighborhood!" When we first moved in, she had invited Kyehwa and me to a Bible study that she and Larry were starting at their home. This became a very important part of my life. Every Tuesday evening, Larry would guide us through the chapter of the Bible for that week, Genesis, in this case. He would ask questions to lead us in conversation and present Power-Point maps and sketches of the places and things we were studying. It made the history come alive! Later, when they moved to Phoenix, and I assumed leadership of the Bible study, I would try to follow in his footsteps but without the Power-Point. We ended up with quite a collection of Old Testament maps of Israel and the Arabian Peninsula.

Chronicles of A Blessed Man

The family arrived at St. Joseph's Hospital on Sunday to find me strapped to the bed and restrained but with the oxygen tube, respirator, and face clamp removed. I was beginning to move around in the bed. The staff had applied the restraints in order to keep me from injuring myself as I thrashed around.

This was apparently when the nightmares had begun. Demons, goblins, and fire repeated over and over again as I began to shake off the effects of the heavy drugs used to induce the coma. I guess I'll never know for sure; I only know it was terrifying.

When the family arrived, the first thing they noticed was that I was straining against the restraints and seemed to be in some pain. I struggled, moaned, and fought against the straps, and there seemed to be something else wrong as well.

"What's the matter with him?" Marina asked the nurse.

"He's all right," came the reply from the med tech. "We just took the respirator out, and he's trying to breathe on his own."

"He's going to wake up! He's going to wake up!" The family was excited but still concerned. I looked as if I were in agony.

"But he's in pain!"

Paul Haber

"That's normal. He's trying to wake up," Nurse Carla told them. "You're distracting him while he's trying to wake up. You guys will have to leave."

My daughter, Ronnie noticed the straps.

"Straps? My dad? You can't strap my dad down! Nobody's going to hold him down! He'll fight until you let him go!" she told them. The staff ignored her. What could she know? She wasn't even a nurse!

In the family, my reputation for being a tough guy was legendary. It's a carry-over from my military career when I always seemed to volunteer for the hardest jobs. At only seventeen, I had joined the Marine Corps right after high school graduation, finished Boot Camp and other training, and promptly volunteered for Force Recon, which was-and is-the elite, Special Operations unit in the Corps.

After Vietnam and completing my four years enlistment, I returned to civilian life for a boring, depressing seven years before returning to the military. I had seventeen jobs and thirteen addresses in that seven years. Initially, I intended to return to the Marines, but when a recruiter told me there was "no way" I could spend my career in Recon, I went next door to the Army recruiter.

Chronicles of A Blessed Man

I only had one question. "What are the odds of my being able to spend the rest of my twenty in either Rangers or Special Forces?"

"No problem," the Sergeant replied.

I was in! I did about three years in the regular Infantry, going from Private to Staff Sergeant, E-6, in only two and a half years. Then I finally got to Special Forces where I "found a home." I completed the challenging Special Forces Qualification Course at age thirty-three and Army Ranger School, nine and a half weeks of one meal and one hour's sleep a day, at the ripe old age of thirty-four. Most Ranger students are in their early twenties.

Then I survived the Special Forces Warrant Officer course at age thirty-eight, becoming one of the first twenty-five candidates chosen for the new position. It was no wonder my kids compared me with the jokes about Chuck Norris!

While Kyehwa returned to the waiting room as ordered, Ronnie and Marina began to investigate. They decided to adjust the blankets over me to try to make me more comfortable. When Marina removed the blankets from the side of the bed, she made a discovery.

"Look!" she cried. "His leg is caught!"

Paul Haber

In my struggles, I had somehow managed to put my leg through the side rails of the bed, and the more I thrashed, the more securely I was hooked. No wonder I was fighting. The girls managed to remove the leg, which seemed to help, but I would not be still.

"There's something you should know about my dad," Marina said. "You can't restrain him. He won't stand for it. He's a fighter!"

"He has to be restrained right now," Carla retorted. "It's for his own safety."

"But he keeps fighting!" Marina returned.

My oldest daughter, Ronnie, got involved, "You've got to release him. He's never stop fighting as long as he's restrained. He'll hurt himself."

The staff continued to refuse to listen until they suddenly discovered my blood pressure had jumped dramatically, getting up into dangerous levels. That changed matters. They disconnected the restraints, my family continued to touch me, talk to me, and I quickly subsided. The blood pressure dropped quickly, and I settled into a fretful semi-sleep as Kyehwa and the girls talked to me.

"Calm, down," they encouraged. "It's for your own good."

Chronicles of A Blessed Man

I quickly complied. I seemed to be much calmer, but I continued to fight against the restraints as Melissa returned to read more scriptures.

CHAPTER 10
"MAKE IT SO, NUMBER ONE!"

"I think it's time," Sue said, doing her best to sound calm and cool. "I think my water broke."

No problem! We had rehearsed the route to the hospital. Besides, this was our first child, and the first one always takes a long time, right?

Nonetheless, I put Sue in the car and broke every speed law the city of Fort Worth, Texas, had in place as I raced to the hospital. We had been monitoring pains, mostly false labor, all day, but we didn't know when the real ones started. But now, it was game time!

I held her arm as we waddled into the emergency room. Fortunately, the place was almost empty, and we were hardly in the door before an alert nurse put two and two together and whisked my wife into a wheel chair and off to the delivery room.

Chronicles of A Blessed Man

Sue and I had been married about fifteen months. She had been barely eighteen, and I was a very immature twenty-one. We mentioned to her folks that we wanted to get married, probably in the local Catholic Church.

Her father had blown his stack! "You will wait at least two years, and you will be married in the church you grew up in!"

Of course, Chuck Sinz had no idea what his tantrum would cause. Sue and I were married a week later with only a few friends in attendance. In fact, I had recently taken a job as a detective in a department store, and Elaine, the officer who trained me, offered her house for the wedding and arranged everything for us. Neither Sue's parents nor mine knew about it for several weeks. My relationship with her parents, not really good to begin with, never recovered.

Several months later, we left upstate New York, where we had both been raised, and moved to Fort Worth, Texas, to follow my dream of a cattle ranch. Even though I had been raised in the East, I had always been a cowboy, riding all my life. I had been thrown from the back of a four-legged cuss when I was only four. No one could remember how old I was for my first ride.

Paul Haber

Unfortunately, our plan to "partner up" with the parents of my Marine Corps buddy didn't work. They were as broke as we were, and there was no way we could afford a ranch that would support two families. I tried carpentry for a while. Amos Howard, my buddy's step-father, was a master carpenter and was willing to train me. Then I got a job at General Dynamics as an aircraft assembler, working on the F111 bomber. It was a great job with good pay and benefits and ended in a 110-man layoff a few weeks before my baby was born.

I was so young, but the cost of the hospital and doctor didn't even enter my mind until it was time to take Sue and the baby, Veronica Lynne Haber, home. What a wake-up call!

But that was still a couple of days in the future. This night, I paced the floor, tried to read magazines, and basically sat in a semi-conscious daze until the nurse came out.

"You have a beautiful daughter," she said.

My heart bounced all around my chest.

"You'll be able to her in a few minutes," she smiled. "Your wife is fine."

In time, Sue had many other children, a total of five with me and more after our divorce. She never had a tough labor. I leaped around the waiting room, like a

Chronicles of A Blessed Man

new heavyweight champion after a knockout win. I had seldom been this happy!

In a little while, the nurse came out with a small bundle wrapped in a pink blanket. When she handed the baby to me, I slid my arms around her smoothly. After all, I was a pro at babies; I had been holding my brother and sisters since I was seven -even babysitting and changing diapers at that age.

I looked down at the sweet little face, and I had a lump in my throat. She was beautiful!

"She looks just like her daddy." The nurse smiled.

"No," I retorted. "She looks like herself, not me or anybody else!" I always did a have a problem with being a little too blunt. I cuddled the little person for a few minutes before giving her back to the nurse. After a brief visit with Sue, I headed back home exhausted, excited, and proud!

Ronnie, as we called her from day one, made an instant change in our lives. From the day we took her home, she would cry all night. She drove me crazy! Of course, the tenser we got, the worse she got, but we all managed to survive the first few months, and the years that followed.

After Sue and I divorced and both remarried, I wanted custody of Ronnie and her four siblings, two each sisters and brothers, but that took four years. Sue would not even allow the kids to visit for several years. Then, one day, while I was attending an Army school in Ft. Benning, Georgia, Sue called out of the blue and asked if I wanted custody of the kids.

I was shocked, to say the least, and instantly suspicious. I soon found that her new husband had left the Army where I had met him and wanted to re-enter, but the recruiter told him "not with six kids." They had another daughter by this time.

After discussing it with Kyehwa, I agreed to take my five children with the proviso that we "make it legal" by going through my lawyer. Sue agreed to that and soon brought the children to Massachusetts to live with us.

Ronnie and her siblings came to live with me and my new wife, Kyehwa. We had only been married a few years and had just had our first baby together, Marina Lee. Suddenly, Kyehwa was "Mom" to five strangers, ranging from thirteen-year-old Ronnie, to Derek, my youngest son, who was six.

Ronnie had spent the previous five years, one year while I was serving in Korea and the subsequent four with her maternal grandparents, Chuck and Margaret (don't call her Maggie!) Sinz. They had never forgiven me for marrying their daughter, which wasn't helped by

Chronicles of A Blessed Man

my "Do it my own way" attitude. They had nothing good to say about me to the girl. Ronnie did not know what to expect!

Suffice to say, Ronnie was spoiled by doting Grandma and Grandpa and was not used to the strict discipline I believed in. Besides that, she weighed less than a hundred pounds while standing five feet four. The Sinzs didn't believe in "forcing the child to eat, if she doesn't want to," so Ronnie was a stick.

Welcome to my world, little girl! Within a couple of years, after massive plates of food, sitting at the table until it was gone, and lots and lots of exercise, she was a beautiful teenager who set high school track records in Massachusetts as well as being an A-B student. We made a lot of mistakes as parents, but some things, we did well.

Unfortunately, she was also very precocious, and we had a lot of "boy trouble" until she finally ran away from our house at seventeen. She went to live with the Sinzs again, but in time, she grew up, met a terrific young man named David Wiese, and got married. They raised three daughters, who are all sweet, gorgeous, and all horse nuts—just like Mom and Grandpa.

Ronnie and David lived in, believe it or not, Box Springs, Georgia, where they actually lived one of my early dreams. They built their home themselves with some help from friends from their church, raised chickens, goats, pigs, and an occasional horse. In addition, David had a full-time job, and they, with their kids, were very much into reenactments, usually specializing in early American history. In fact, Ronnie was working in Westville, a reenactment town in Georgia. Ronnie had always teased that she would always be my "Number One" like the Executive Officer in Star Trek: The Next Generation; the years hadn't changed that.

So, you can understand my surprise when I realized that was really her standing near my bed in ICU.

CHAPTER 11
LAZARUS AWAKES

The goblins, demons, and gargoyles continued to chase me across the blasted and tortured landscape as flames shot up from mounds in the earth, threatening to engulf me as I ran endlessly in mortal fear.

No matter which way I ran, something was there blocking my path as I dodged and ducked their grasping claws. I screamed and prayed as I fought my way free of their grip, but they could fly faster than I could run. There was no escape.

Suddenly, the scene changed but still made no sense. I was lying on my back in a strange room I had never seen before, looking up at three women I didn't recognize. Their faces were huge—bloated, expanded, and with a strange brown tint. They all had long hair and all were showing their teeth. I think they were supposed to be smiling, but at the time—after the ghouls and devils—I wasn't sure. For just a second, I was afraid they were going to eat me.

"Dad! Dad, are you awake?" the one on the left asked.

The monster's face was long and wide with a strange shade of brown skin, dark brown hair, and large teeth. It was strange. The teeth weren't the pointed fangs, designed for slashing, that I had been seeing on the other creatures chasing me. This one had teeth like Mr. Ed (the horse on the old TV show), and the shape of its face kept changing as if it were a balloon filled with water, pulsing and shifting with any movement.

The one on the left said, "Hi, Dad!"

Huh? She had big teeth but the voice sounded kind of familiar—like I had heard it once, a long time ago.

"Who are you?" I croaked, trying to speak around the obstruction. I felt some sort of a stick, I thought, in my throat. What the heck was that doing there?

"Dad, it's me, Ronnie!"

I knew the creature was lying to me. Ronnie was in Georgia. I hadn't seen her in several years, so she couldn't be here. My suspicions grew. Who were these people pretending to be someone I knew? What did they want from me? Where they demons coming to take my soul? Not if I could help it.

Chronicles of A Blessed Man

"No, you're lying!" The voice coming out of my throat was unrecognizable, harsh, and husky as if coated in coal dust. That couldn't be my voice. What had happened?

"It's true, Dad," the second apparition spoke. "I'm Alicia!"

Nope! Alicia was in Texas. Who the heck were these people? Besides, my daughters didn't have this strange, muddy brown skin and hair, and were certainly not as huge as the apparitions I was gazing at. Their faces looked kind of like balloons and were kind of lumpy. Were they demons standing in front of me?

"You're lying! I don't believe you," I said.

The third goblin, the one on the right, said, "Dad, it is true! I'm Marina."

Now, I knew for sure they were fakes. I had just seen Marina a few minutes ago. She drove me…somewhere! I couldn't really remember where it was we went, but it was just a little while ago. Besides, Marina didn't look like the apparition in front of me, at least, not much. Each of these imposters vaguely resembled someone I used to know, but I just couldn't focus on the memory. Certainly, they couldn't be my daughters!

Now, I understood. These creatures, these servants of the devil, were using the names of my loved ones, my daughters, to convince me to go along quietly to their headquarters in Hell.

"I don't believe you," I snapped. They weren't going to take me without a fight even if I couldn't move my arms at the moment. What was wrong with my arm anyway?

They continued to try to convince me, but I wasn't buying it; they couldn't be my beautiful daughters, not with the huge round faces and strange coloring. Besides, Ronnie lived in Georgia and Alicia was in Texas. Why would they be here? And the voices…they sounded sort of familiar, but they weren't quite right. My daughters didn't sound like that. It was a trick!

"No, you're lying. Go away!" They might be able to take me to whatever place they came from, but I wasn't going willingly.

Then, I caught a movement on my left and turned my head to see the new threat. Strange! This one had shorter, darker hair than the others and almond- shaped eyes. She looked like someone I knew, but I couldn't remember who. She had Asian eyes! Kyehwa had eyes like that!

Suddenly, I knew! Even though her features were swollen like these goblins in front of me, this was someone I could trust, whoever she was.

Chronicles of A Blessed Man

"I believe her," I rasped, trying to get my eyes to focus. The Asian lady smiled. That was all right, but I didn't trust the smiles on the other three. Was this a new trick?

Then it really got weird. The one that looked kind of like my wife stood in front of me and began to explain that I had had surgery and… Wait a minute! I didn't have any surgery planned. What surgery? Why couldn't I remember anything before I woke up a few minutes ago? Was I in the hospital?

Why? How? The only thing I remembered was that a long time ago, before the devils and the flames, I had planned a trip to California. I had surgery two years ago, but nothing recent that I could remember.

Incidentally, it was two weeks later before I finally got all this straight. At that moment, I was a sick, confused man with something sticking out of my nose that seemed to go all the way down my throat. It hurt to talk, it hurt to swallow, and nothing made any sense at all.

"I'm here. I'm here," she said, touching me, rubbing my arms, and scratching my head. Then the newcomer held something to my ear. "It's Melissa," she said. Melissa? Where was Melissa?

Paul Haber

The thing at my ear must be a cell phone, but where in the world was Melissa, and why was she calling me? Why in the world would I want to talk to my youngest daughter, Melissa, right now? And why was she on the phone? Where was I, and where was she? Melissa and her husband, Kern, live in Orlando. Why was she on the cell phone? What was going on around here?

"You stinker!" The voice on the phone was sobbing. "You had to wait until I left to wake up, you stinker!"

Melissa, who I found out later, had been at my side since arriving from Orlando on Friday night, had to be at work on Tuesday, and had only an hour or so before gone to the airport, disappointed that I had not awakened. After traveling so far to give me love and to support her mother, she was forced to return without being able to see me awake. No sooner did Kyehwa return from dropping her off Melissa got a call, saying I was awake. Stinker, indeed!

CHAPTER 12
MISS MELISS

When we found out that Kyehwa was pregnant again, it couldn't have been a more difficult time. I had just been commissioned as an Army Warrant Officer, and for some reason, thought it was time to move off base and enter the civilian sector. The small pay raise I received did not come close to handling the increased cost of living such as rent, utilities, a longer commute, and so forth. Living on base for several years had allowed me to become spoiled; I forgot the myriad expenses I avoided in government quarters.

Kyehwa had returned to work instead of being at home as a full-time mom. We had found in the past that it was better to have her available in case a kid got sick at school or some other such crisis. She had been forced to quit several jobs in order to handle such stuff since I was gone most of the time. It was almost as if she were a single mom, raising six children all by herself. The only difference was that once every couple of weeks or months, I would show up to be husband and father, which was more of an intrusion than any real assistance. When I was home, I spent any free time I had with the kids, either teaching them martial arts or cutting the firewood we used to heat the house. We couldn't afford the high electric bills to do that job. Kyehwa and her needs were largely ignored.

While she carried Melissa, she was actually holding down two jobs, night shift closer at a Burger King and an early morning paper route that required her to be up and at the publisher at two AM every day.

To make things worse, we were living in New England. It was winter, and there was ice all over the ground. One early morning, she slipped on the ice and took a fall. She didn't mention it for several days until she began to notice spots of blood on her underwear. I insisted she see a doctor, and we found she was in danger of losing the baby.

The rest of the pregnancy was tough on her and the entire family. It finally penetrated my head that I needed to be more helpful. She was in and out of the hospital on bed rest, we needed the money the paper route brought in, so we found a way to continue. Since I was not deployed at the time, I would get up at about one AM,

Chronicles of A Blessed Man

wake up one or two of the kids, and we would handle the paper route, sometimes with Kyehwa driving and sometimes it was me. I don't know how the children handled it while going to school. I was exhausted!

Finally, it was time for the baby to arrive. Kyehwa had told the OB/GYN that she wanted to deliver vaginally despite having our previous daughter, Marina, by Caesarean. The doctor agreed to try it even though it was unusual. The labor pains, confused with false labor and other things going on for so long, finally progressed to the point that Kyehwa was admitted to the delivery room. I didn't think she knew what she had asked for, and for several hours, I was proved right. The pain was intense, and my wife, who usually considered the word "damn" as a serious curse, cussed me out like the proverbial sailor. It was all my fault and so on…

She told me later that if she had delivered Marina normally, there would not have been another child. I could imagine. I have never been able to understand how a woman could deal with that much pain, but they've been doing it forever.

Once again, I held the baby first; Kyehwa was exhausted and in pain, and for just a few minutes, didn't want any part of this newcomer. That quickly passed, but not until I had a chance to whisper in Melissa's ear how welcomed she was and how much she was loved.

The entire family loved and spoiled her as much as any child in our family got spoiled. But even as a small child, she was quite sensitive. When I would raise my voice to shout at one of her sisters, which happened more often than I like to admit, Melissa would start to cry. Then, I would shout at her and say, "If you're going to cry, go to bed!"

After a short while, she would avoid all the grief by going to her bed as soon as I entered the house. This became especially noticeable when we were in Korea. I guess Melissa was about four, and it suddenly dawned on me that she was terrified of me, of my temper, and of my noise when I was angry. Since I seemed to be angry every day, the little one was usually unhappy once "Daddy" came home.

I discussed this with Kyehwa, and for once, listened to what she had to say. I knew I needed to reconnect with Melissa and decided to do it through a form of bribery.

At first, I would buy an Ice cream cone from the Korean store near our house, bring it home and almost beg her to take it. She was so afraid of me that she wouldn't even come close for the treat. Eventually, she

Chronicles of A Blessed Man

would come to me, and we convinced her to meet me at the door. The next step was to actually step outside the small compound we lived in and go to the store to pick out her ice cream. It worked.

After several weeks, we had become friends again. We would go for long walks around the section of Seoul called Nam San, South Mountain, one of the hills the city was built on. We would walk hand-in-hand, and as frequently happened, some Korean mother would comment on how beautiful she was; Melissa would answer in her flawless Hangul.

If one of the ladies would speak to me, Melissa would translate, "She said it costs one hundred Won, Daddy." I always thought it was funny that my baby spoke better Korean than I did, and I was supposed to be a Liaison officer!

When we returned to the States and settled in Tucson, Melissa attended her first public, non-military, school. It wasn't long before her teacher called Kyehwa and asked for a meeting.

She was concerned, she said, because she felt Melissa needed speech therapy; she couldn't speak English. When asked to speak in class, Melissa seemed to speak in gibberish. The problem was that, at home, we spoke English, Korean, German, a little Japanese, and some

Spanish. We frequently mixed them up and played word games with them. The little girl thought that was normal, so she continued it at school.

Kyehwa soon demonstrated to the teacher that it was she- the teacher- who couldn't speak enough languages to understand. Nevertheless, Melissa was so traumatized and embarrassed that she refused to speak anything other than English for many years.

Now Melissa was grown and calling me a stinker.

I have no idea what I said on the phone or even if I said anything. But I had a warm glow that she had come all this way for me! Then it hit me. If that were really Melissa, if the Asian lady was really Kyehwa, maybe the other three were really my daughters as they said. No, too weird, couldn't be! I directed my question to the one who had spoken first.

"Who are you?"

"I'm your daughter, Ronnie."

"Why are you here?"

"You almost died! You had surgery."

"You lie," I drawled slowly. My mouth, like my brain, seemed to be operating in slow motion. "Why are you lying?"

"No, really, Dad. You've been sick."

Chronicles of A Blessed Man

It didn't compute. Why were they here wherever "here" was? Why was I here?"

Kyehwa retuned with a wet paper towel and began to wipe my face.

"What are you doing?" I managed to ask, trying to get away.

"Shut up," she ordered. "I'm wiping your face."

Light dawned. That really was my wife! No one else ordered my around like that. Maybe what they were telling me was true.

"Ow!" I moaned, looking up at her where she was standing on my left.

"What's the matter?"

"Ow!" The word seemed to take forever to get out. The pain in my left arm was intense, and I couldn't understand it. It was hours later before I realized the pain and pressure was caused by the blood pressure cuff on my left arm, operating automatically every half hour.

I began to cough, it felt as if there were a stick caught in my throat. What had happened to me?

The one I thought might be Kyehwa leaned over me. "Did you see God?" she asked.

I have no idea why I answered as I did. "Yeah."

"What did he tell you?"

"Not yet," I told her.

Paul Haber

"Not yet? You're not going to tell me?"

I made a face. "He said 'not yet'," I explained.

Someone else approached. His head was enlarged like all the others, but he, too, looked familiar.

"How are you feeling?" he asked.

"Who are you?"

"I'm Travis. I came to see you." Travis is my son-in-law, famous for showing up at odd times, usually with ice cream or beer. But he was supposed to be in Texas with his wife, Alicia.

"Why?" I asked just before I started another coughing fit.

I must have grossed him out because he left, and the apparition who said she was Marina returned.

"Dad, this is Marina."

I tried to nod. "Why am I here?"

"Cause you're sick," she answered.

That couldn't be, I didn't remember being sick. "You're lying!" I told her. It seemed to be the only answer I could give.

Alicia and Travis returned. It was like they were coming in relays. What…?

"Who are you?" I asked, still not sure.

"I'm Alicia."

Chronicles of A Blessed Man

Could it be true? Did they come all the way from Waco? I was still confused. "Why are you here?" I asked, hoping for a clearer answer.

"You're sick."

"You're lying. I'm not sick."

Marina spoke up, "Yeah, you are! If you didn't want to cut my grass, you could have just said so."

I remembered that I had planned to cut some of the acres of high grass at her house. I also had a strange impish feeling, so I held up my hand with the middle finger extended.

"Did you shoot me the bird?" she asked, laughing. I just smiled, sort of.

"You're ornery, aren't you?" Kyehwa and the girls laughed among themselves.

"Why are you laughing?" I quizzed.

"We're laughing because we're happy! You're waking up!"

"Why?" I just couldn't seem to understand what had happened.

Marina answered, "Don't you remember? You didn't want to cut my grass, so you went to the hospital."

I looked to Alicia. "Can I shoot her the bird?" I asked.

Paul Haber

She grinned. "Well, in this circumstance, why not? She deserves it."

I did. After Marina slapped my hand for flipping her off, everybody smiled—even me.

What seemed to be a few moments later, the phone was back. "It's PJ," said the Asian lady.

Now, this voice I actually recognized. My oldest son has an accent I always tease him about—hillbilly is what I call it, but I guess it is closer to Southern Redneck, since he's lived in Alabama and North Carolina for years, but hillbilly is easier. Besides, I know it irritates him. At any rate, I knew his voice but still didn't know why he was calling, or had we called him? It seemed a very important question at that moment. Why? I don't know. I was so very, very tired.

Again, I don't know what either of us said, but I felt a little better. At least, I was beginning to believe the three women who claimed to be my daughters, so I had spoken to five of my seven kids. Now if someone would just explain…

I went back to sleep.

My eyes opened a minute (?) later. Alicia and Travis were standing near the bed again along with Kyehwa. Where do these people keep disappearing to?

Chronicles of A Blessed Man

"The kids are outside," my bride told me, "Katie and Cameron. They can't come in."

I could picture Cameron, but Katie? I must know more than one Katie because I was very confused.

"Katie? Who's Katie?" I asked.

Alicia spoke up, "Katie. My Katie."

Oh, yeah, Alicia and Travis's daughter. I remember now. Boy, my head was full of cotton!

I looked hard at Travis. "You're big!" I told him, referring to how swelled up his head and body looked to me. He misunderstood my meaning, thinking I was talking about his weight.

"Yeah," he replied, "I need to lose some weight."

I couldn't figure out how he could lose all the swelling. Wasn't that part of him? Everybody was big, but he just looked bigger, probably because he's over six feet tall. I didn't know how to say what I was thinking, so I let it go. I tried to explain later, but I don't think he understood.

Paul Haber

CHAPTER 13
TALL, DARK AND TRAVIS

"Dad, this is Travis."

This tall, skinny guy was not Alicia's first boyfriend. She had even been pretty serious about one before, but that one hadn't "made the cut" past high school graduation. She was beautiful enough to turn heads. She had even taken a shot at modeling.

But Travis Roberson was the first one she's brought home to meet me; I had just rejoined the family after retiring from the Army. Travis, I found, was a crew member on EC-130 airplanes for the Air Force. The" E" in the designation stood for Electronic for gathering intelligence to be used by our armed forces.

He seemed like a pretty sharp kid, very quick-witted. That would come in handy if he were going to hang around our family. "Come back quick or die!" could have been one of our family mottos.

Chronicles of A Blessed Man

I don't remember what started the conversation, but testosterone was rampant. This young buck facing the not-so-old bull. I remember sitting in a rocking chair when Travis delivered a slightly disrespectful line. I cocked my head and continued rocking.

"That's right, old man. You just stay in your rocker!" Snap!

I came out of the chair in a flash, and he turned to run away- too slow! My hands gripped his collar on both sides of his neck from behind and quickly applied pressure on the carotid artery with the sides of both thumbs. He struggled for maybe two seconds, then he dropped like a stone. I caught him before he hit the floor. Never insult a fifth-degree black belt even in fun.

I let him sleep for a few seconds while both Kyehwa and Alicia expressed their unhappiness with me, then I applied some Kappo resuscitation techniques, and he quickly woke up. Despite this rocky start, Travis soon became a favorite at our house and married Alicia a few months later.

Travis had been raised in Nevada and a few other places. His parents had divorced along the way, and Travis was raised by his mother. According to the stories, he was something of a scamp. In one instance, he wrestled his younger brother to the ground then grabbed his collar and hung him on a nail in the wall.

According to both his mother and Travis himself, he was always getting in trouble, nothing really evil, just very hyper boy stuff. He managed to keep it together enough to graduate high school and enlisted in the Air force. He hadn't been stationed at Davis Monthan Air Force Base in Tucson very long when he went to the movies and met…Alicia.

It didn't seem like it was very long before their Katie was born, and everything seemed to be going okay. For a while, they lived in an apartment just around the corner from our home, so we got to see them quite often.

Immaturity and stubbornness on both sides caused them some trouble after a year or so, and after giving birth to their daughter, Katie, ended up divorcing. For several months, Travis would come to us for advice and counsel. We really felt he was the victim in the divorce; we discussed strategy. He really loved Alicia and we watched with crossed fingers while he pursued her again.

They had originally married quickly without inviting either family, we had hopes that they would reconcile and put the past behind them.

Chronicles of A Blessed Man

Whatever strategy Travis used worked. He and Alicia remarried awhile later and were raising Katie and two sons, Ryan and Cameron, together. Travis traveled a lot for his Air Force job and frequently would show up at our door unexpected but always welcome. He invariable had a bag of ice cream, or a six-pack of cold beer in his hand when he knocked at our door. It became a running gag in our family. Although they were living in various places, he would fly in to Davis Monthan Air Force Base in Tucson and always made our house one of his first stops- he said it was to get good Korean food.

In return, we called him our favorite son-in-law- a long way from being the "pencil-necked geek" I had named him early on in our relationship. Travis was, at that time, still in the Air Force, but several promotions and transfers had taken them first to Edwards Air Force Base near Palmdale, California, then to Waco, Texas. His job had changed, and he was working with some retired Special Operations types, some of whom were old associates of mine, and other kinds of "spooks." When I asked him what he was doing, he came back with the old line I used to use that was a famous retort in Special Ops.

"If I told you, I'd have to kill you."

Paul Haber

I really love that wise guy! But what was he doing at my bedside? Kyehwa came back, playing with my hair and…what the heck? My beard. I never wear a beard. Where did that come from?

"I have long hair," I croaked.

"A beard too," she replied. "I never saw you with a beard before. You look just like Mike."

Mike Reynolds was my friend and a martial arts student of over 10 years. With a six-foot-something frame carrying close to 300 pounds, he wore a full beard and bushy red hair. Did I look that hairy?

Kyehwa continued," I'm going to braid your hair."

Oh, oh! Déjà vu! That was part of the hallucinations I had had before.

"You said that!" I told her. Didn't she remember?

Time moved in jerky moments. The clock on the wall didn't seem to move at all, and then it would jump a half hour even though I swore I hadn't been asleep.

Suddenly, I saw someone I recognized. Collen Donovan, the young girl I called my favorite blonde. She was the daughter of a former co-worker and friend named Sandra Perfetto, and had been another of my students off and on for several years. She had even rented a room from us for a semester of college. But today, she had the same problem as everybody else. her

Chronicles of A Blessed Man

corn-silk hair was darker, kind of a muddy brown, and she looked kind of inflated. What the…

"I came to see you," she said.

"You look weird!" I told her. Never accuse me of having manners or tact.

"Yeah, I am kind of weird," she said sadly. She had misinterpreted my meaning, and I had hurt her feelings.

Kyehwa intervened, "It's his eyes. He's having trouble seeing."

I hoped Collen understood. I wouldn't hurt her for the world. I kept trying to focus my eyes as if that would help. But nothing changed. Everything was distorted, and even the furnishings of my room looked funny colors and shapes…

CHAPTER 14
MY FAVORITE BLONDE

"Hajime!"

The referee moved quickly out of the way but almost not quickly enough. The pretty blonde teen-ager in the white karate uniform launched across the three-foot space toward her opponent, who was a twenty-something guy several inches taller and a few pounds heavier.

Hands and feet flying, she drove him backward as he panicked and ran away from her attack—out of the fighting area.

There had been no other teen-aged girls her size and rank, so the powers-that-be for the tournament had scheduled her to fight young men they considered appropriate. The girl, Collen, was a little nervous about that until the command to begin! Then her training and

Chronicles of A Blessed Man

natural aggressiveness took over, and she went at her opponent like a whirlwind of fists and feet.

She won three straight times that day to take the blue ribbon for her class, and she did it by completely overwhelming all three opponents; not one of them scored a single point on her.

Collen (pronounced as Colleen) Donovan was born in Phoenix, Arizona, in 1989, daughter of Jim and Sandra Donovan.

With her parents, she moved to "the land," some country property near Concho, Arizona, where they lived with no electricity or running water. There were several moves over the next couple of years, but she was too young to remember most of them.

Later, after her parents separated, she, with her mother and two older brothers, moved to Winslow, then St. Johns, and finally, Tucson. This is where she entered my life.

I had met Collen's mother, Sandra (now Perfetto), in the course of my job at the Department of Corrections but didn't meet Collen for a couple of years. One day, Sandra mentioned that her middle-school-aged daughter had expressed an interest in learning self-defense.

Since Sandra knew I was an instructor and lived nearby, she asked me if I would teach her daughter. I agreed, met Collen, and fell in love with the young girl almost immediately. She tended to be a little shy and had some self-esteem issues but was one of the sweetest kids I had ever met.

She joined my class for a while, quit for a brief period, and sometime during her eighth-grade year, returned to the dojo for three or four more years. During that time, her family had moved back to Willcox, Arizona, some seventy miles away, but as soon as Collen got her driver's license, she began driving into Tucson once or twice a week for class.

After she graduated from high school and received a partial scholarship to the University of Arizona in Tucson, it was only logical that she stay with Kyehwa and me while she attended college. Our daughters had grown and moved out, leaving plenty of room. While Collen studied Anthropology and practiced karate, she found the time to work for Kyehwa in our tailor shop. She had simply become part of the family.

Over the next few years, she struggled with growing up, seeking her independence, and having too much fun partying with her friends, but managed to hold down a job at a local Olive Garden as a server. She also grew in poise and self-confidence as well as becoming even more beautiful. Over those years, up until today, one

Chronicles of A Blessed Man

thing never changed- she was always my favorite blonde.

I couldn't tell you what else we talked about, but I know I had trouble hearing her soft voice without my hearing aids. It was a great treat to see her even without my glasses. It had been a month or two since I had seen her. She stayed to visit for a while. I guess that meant someone else had gone to the waiting room, but I figured that out much later.

Time seemed to be flexible. It stood still when I was alone and jumped in long leaps when I was occupied with visitors. Sometime during this millennium, a familiar shadow blocked the light. This one, I recognized without any trouble. It could only be one person, big (inflated to be bigger than normal like everybody else I looked at that day), bushy hair and beard. It could only be the "Red Bear" himself, Mike Reynolds.

"Hey," I said.

"Good morning," he greeted me in his usual style. "How are ya feeling?"

I tried to smile, but it must have looked grotesque. "I feel like crap. You're the first one I recognize," I told him.

That seemed to please him. Mike had just come from teaching the martial arts class we participate in every

Paul Haber

Monday and Friday. Now, suddenly, I knew what day it was- Monday Up until then, I wasn't sure. It felt like Saturday for some reason.

Chronicles of A Blessed Man

CHAPTER 15
THE NOT-SO-CUDDLY BEAR

I met Mike Reynolds when he was a Captain, and I, a Corrections Officer. He was my boss's boss for about two weeks until I was promoted to Sergeant and transferred to another unit.

We hooked up again about a year and a half later when, after returning to Tucson complex, I was assigned to be the Disciplinary Sergeant for Santa Rita Unit, and Mike was the Disciplinary Coordinator for the Tucson complex, some eight units.

My job was to process the "ticket" or disciplinary report, determining if they were a minor or major infraction, and if major, to refer them to the Coordinator for judgment. The Coordinator was sort of a judge but handling only disciplinary matters; real crimes were handled by the District Attorney.

Paul Haber

Mike would examine the ticket, the inmate's past disciplinary record, and any evidence that might apply. Then he would interview the offender and either, infrequently, drop the charges or impose sanctions, according to Department of Corrections' policy. He had some leeway, so a frequent offender would receive tougher sanctions than one who generally stayed out of trouble.

Working together gave us a chance to get to know each other, and I found Captain Reynolds to be amazingly gentle for a big man. He was over six feet and close to three hundred pounds. Even as a Captain, he always wore a full beard, and with his red hair, resembled nothing so much as a big bear. In fact, that was his personal "totem" or symbol. I also found he had an interest in the martial arts and had studied Kempo at one period as a young man.

It didn't take long for Mike to sign up for my class, and in time, become a black belt and my senior student.

I guess Mike's biggest challenge in my class was to learn the Japanese terms for everything. My instructor, or Sensei, had been very traditional, and I tried to follow his example. In addition, right at the beginning of the training, I required my students to memorize a rather long and detailed history/ legend of the founding of the

Chronicles of A Blessed Man

martial arts, especially our style, Kajukenbo. Many new students were intimidated and quit rather than learn it.

But Mike plugged away at it and put up with my rather strict methods. By this time, he had been studying with me for about thirteen years and was a highly skilled practitioner and instructor.

It was uncanny sometimes while he was teaching one of his Kohai, or student junior to him, I could almost hear me talking with his voice. He had learned to mimic my language, my style…everything. He learned well, was diligent, loyal, and one of my very best friends. He remains so to this day.

Mike lived a good distance out in the desert, about ten miles or so east of the Marana exit on Interstate 10. During most of the year, the road was no problem, but during the summer Monsoon rains in July and August, four-wheel drive was mandatory. Mike's SUV was always covered with a thick coat of red mud especially at this time of the year. He usually only made the trip into Tucson on work days. For him, that was Friday through Sunday. For this reason, we had scheduled our classes for Monday and Friday evenings.

As usual, I can't remember what we talked about other than Marlo, a student Mike called "Boy Blunder," because of his propensity to get rattled in times of stress.

Paul Haber

Mike hung around for a brief while then left to drive home—over forty miles. Imagine, he had detoured that far just to visit. That cut through the confusion and touched me deeply.

It gave me a feeling of being important, of being cherished, every time someone showed up at my bedside. Mike had gone out of his way to cover my class then came to the hospital, even though he lived in the opposite direction. I thought of my family flying in from Florida and Georgia, driving from Texas, spending the day with me while their own families were left on their own, in some cases, with ill or injured family members in the home.

Sometime later that day, while Kyehwa wiped the saliva from my mouth and wet my lips and tongue with a sponge-stick because I couldn't have water yet.

"I'm tired," I complained.

"Why are you tired? Do you know how long you've been sleeping?"

I only knew how exhausted I felt. "I'm tired. I need to sleep," I told her.

"You had surgery. They had to put you down."

Put me down? Like a horse or a dog? What? It didn't matter at that point. "I love you," I told her. "You're beautiful."

Chronicles of A Blessed Man

She told me later I must be getting better. I was "buttering her up." I only vaguely remember saying goodnight, and the nurse put something in my IV. I went to sleep again.

CHAPTER 16
THE WALL AND THE LESSON

I don't know how long I slept. I only knew that I was taking a great dislike to that wall. Centered on it was a white board where the nurse and med tech wrote their names for each shift. It was too dark to read, which, of course, made reading it crucial to me for some reason.

Above and to the left, as I faced it, was a small crucifix, and above the board was that blasted clock, the one that never seemed to move until I had a visitor. Then it would jump forward.

I know I slept a little, but I stared at the clock most of the night. 3:00, 3:30, 4:00, etc., etc., for the long, interminable night. Except for the board, there was nothing else to look at, and I was propped up in bed with God only knows how many pillows. I could only move marginally, and even then, my left arm was secured with a blood-pressure cuff, which would automatically trigger every time I dozed off. Actually, I discovered later that it was set for every thirty minutes, and hurt! Until I discovered what was causing the pain every short while, I thought I was having a heart attack or something—very scary and very frustrating.

Finally, after what was surely the longest night of my life, the lights came on marginally, and a young black woman, a med tech, entered and scrawled two names on the board. Hers was Tolu. I thought I remembered her from the day before when I had awakened. Her bright red smock had been the only patch of bright color that hadn't looked contaminated with the brown shade that seemed to cover everything and everyone.

Today, her smock looked different but still a kind of bright red-orange shade.

"Tolu. Is that your name?" I asked. That stick was still in my throat. What the…? It made it almost impossible to speak.

"That's me." She smiled.

"Do you always wear red?'

"Do I always wear red? No, I wore red yesterday, but this is orange."

I had to think about that for a minute, and by then, she was gone about her other duties.

Kyehwa arrived, smiling.

Paul Haber

I greeted her with my most romantic line, "I hate that wall!" Okay, not very romantic, but that's what was on my mind.

"Why do you hate that wall?" she asked.

"It's ugly, and the clock doesn't work," I replied.

She seemed delighted that I was awake enough to notice that the dog-gonned clock was malfunctioning. Who ever heard of clock that went forward, backward, and stopped on its own?

Alicia and Travis came in to say goodbye. They had a fourteen-hour drive back to Waco. After I had thanked them for coming, Alicia said, "You know, Dad, if you want me to come see you, just ask. You don't have to go to the hospital."

How come all my kids are smart-alecks? I think I smiled, "Why are you here anyway?"

"You had surgery."

"What surgery?"

"Your stomach," Ali said patiently as if talking to a small, not-very-bright child.

"What about my stomach?" I knew it hurt, but I was so wrapped up that I hadn't even seen the bandages.

Kyehwa explained once again about me getting sick, being operated on, almost dying, being operated on again, and…what…?

Chronicles of A Blessed Man

It all made no sense to me. I had absolutely no recent memory before I woke up in this bed. I remembered a week or so before. It seemed like yesterday but nothing about how I got into this predicament.

About then, Ronnie came in and took a picture of me to send via cell phone to another daughter Cori, my son Paul, and Ronnie's daughter Becka. I have no idea what was so appealing about me lying in that bed, but everybody seemed to enjoy it—except me. Lying around is not my favorite thing, but it seemed to be important to everybody that I did so. Plus, I was strapped down!

Tolu came back in and cranked me be up to a sitting position in order to keep my lungs drained, she said. It did help. I had been having a little difficulty with congestion and mucus during the night.

Ronnie looked at me and chuckled. "You look like an elephant," she said.

I didn't think that was very nice until later when I saw a picture of me with the tube sticking out of my nose—more like a rhino.

"I hate that wall," I complained. Ronnie came immediately to the rescue. She did a little dance in front of the offending furnishings. The wall didn't change.

"It's still there," I told her. Everybody seemed delighted by my observation. I didn't get it.

Paul Haber

Someone brought in a chair for me to sit in. If I could successfully sit in the chair, I could go to a room, get out of ICU, and away from that wall! Give me that chair!

Only one problem. I couldn't do it. Kyehwa tried to help but was not strong enough.

Tolu came to assist, and Ronnie got into the act. Between the two of them, they grasped me under the arms and got me out of bed. They hauled me like a sack of flour with legs getting in the way. Whatever had hit me, maybe a truck, had done something to my legs. Just…yesterday? I was running and doing lunges up a hill. At this point, the weakness bothered me more than anything. I wasn't old yet.

"Okay, Dad," Ronnie said easily as if I weighed nothing at all. "We're going to move you to your chair."

Well, that was easy! Not!

Sometime around noon, according to the infernal clock, as I was sitting hunched and semi-comfortably in the chair, someone decided it was time to improve my posture.

"Pick your head up, Mister Haber." I didn't know who the trouble-maker was, but couldn't she just leave me alone? I was doing fine, just slumped over here, almost bent double.

Chronicles of A Blessed Man

Then Ronnie decided to bother me again. Why is it that the first child is the most troublesome? They think it's their right or something, I guess. She pushed me forward in the chair a little just enough for her to get me in a bear-hug and lift me to my feet. My head was still hanging on my chest.

"Look up, Dad," she commanded.

I knew I might as well comply. She thought she was in charge here anyway. I struggled to look up directly into a round, white, very bright light.

"What do you see, Dad?"

I knew the answer to this one! "A light," I answered.

"You know what? You just had a spiritual lesson. Look up!"

"I hate lessons!" This standing job was so tough—especially trying to lift my hundred-pound head. I rested it on Ronnie's forehead for a while.

After what seemed an hour, she let me sit down again. "Are you in pain?" she asked.

What the heck did she think? "Duh!"

Ronnie was insistent," On a scale of one to ten, what's your pain level?"

I thought about that for a while. "Two."

I saw her smile. "Our level 2 or theirs?"

Paul Haber

I knew she was referring to the philosophy I had taught her years before. Habers didn't feel pain as much as "normal" people. We were special, unique, and maybe weird, at least not very bright about pain.

"Ours," I told her.

"About a seven on theirs then," she nodded, chuckling.

I nodded. I figured that was about right.

As Ronnie and Kyehwa talked, I heard something that bothered me. Ronnie's husband was in the hospital back home in Georgia. What? David Wiese was sick, and his wife was here?

I looked at her. "Go home!"

Kyehwa responded, "That's not nice!"

I realized she had misunderstood my meaning. I looked at Ronnie. "Go home to husband."

Ronnie shook her head and bent closer. "David said "this is where I belong," she told me softly.

That choked me up so badly, I couldn't even argue. "Thank you," I croaked.

Several hours later, Kyehwa says about four PM, my face got very white. I was so exhausted, and my head just wouldn't stop drooping, no matter how much of my super-human strength I tried to use.

"You need to go back to bed," Kyehwa told me.

Chronicles of A Blessed Man

"No!" The thought terrified me!

Ronnie leaned toward me. "Dad, are you sure?"

"I'm not going back to bed."

Ronnie was insistent, "You look very tired. You need to get back in bed."

"No! I hate that wall!" Didn't they understand? I argued with the two of them for a while. Finally, I tried to explain, "If I get back in bed, they won't move me to the other room. No bed!"

They tried for several minutes to convince me that it was okay to get back in bed, but I knew the truth. I had to sit in the chair if I wanted to get out of ICU. The nurse had told me that when they put me in the chair. No way was the wall and that…that…clock going to win!

Kyehwa went out. When she came back, she told me she had talked to the nurse, and it was all right to get back in bed.

She couldn't fool me! I knew the rules. "No! I hate that wall!"

Finally, somebody, I'm not sure who, brought another staff member. We still argue about whether it was a tech or a nurse. "Mister Haber, I'm sorry. Your nurse is busy, but it's okay to get back in bed. You'll still get out of ICU. You're just waiting for a room to be open."

Paul Haber

Somebody, I was too "wiped out" to notice who, helped me into the bed.

"Thank God! I'm so tired!"

"That's my dad," Ronnie told the staff member. "You can't tell him what to do. If you restrain him, he'll fight. If you want him to be still, you have to calm him down"

I settled into the bed, propped by pillows on every side, and felt myself drift into that limbo. My body was asleep while the mind remained awake. My family left, and about seven pm, I got "sprung" from ICU and moved to 2 South, room 215. I was only half-awake, but I was victorious! I was getting away from the wall and that clock!

CHAPTER 17
THE NICE-ER GUY

They wheeled me into the room, and I lay like a sack of something while three people slid my half-conscious body from the gurney to the bed. I noticed the really important things. The wall was different. I couldn't say exactly how, and the television was playing sports, I think. I also noticed that the tech working to set up my IV was young and quite pretty. I guess the older I get, the younger others seem.

I could hear someone in the other bed, moving quietly rustling the sheets, changing the position of the mattress, and so on. A roommate. As the staff left, I lay propped by who knows how many pillows in my bed. I guess I could have moved, but they had me pretty well wedged in for the moment. Of course, that meant I was flat on my back, bed cranked up a little, and facing directly into the TV with ESPN flashing pictures of exciting football highlights. At least, they would have been exciting if I had been at all interested, but I was so tired! At least, the sound was turned down, so I didn't have to listen to it too. The light from the picture flashed through my eyelids, but I managed to ignore it for a while.

I tried to sleep, but my eyes wouldn't stay closed, partly because of the television, I guess, but also because my sleep pattern was kind of messed up. I still couldn't get straight in my head what day it was or how long I had been unconscious. Was it one day since I got sick or two? I didn't realize at the time that it had been a week since I had collapsed in pain.

When the nurse, also young and quite pretty, (yes, I would notice that, wouldn't I?) came in, I asked her if it were possible to close the curtain since I really needed to sleep. The clock now said it was after eleven. She complied, and I heard her speaking softly to my "roomie." In a few moments, she came back to my side and told me that the other guy had decided that he needed to get some sleep too since he was going home in the morning. I felt envy and relief. How long until I could go home?

Chronicles of A Blessed Man

Soon, it was darker in the room; there was just enough light to make out shadows, and I settled in for the night and lay there awake for what seemed two days. I must have slept, but since I couldn't see the clock through the curtains, I couldn't tell whether time was passing or not. First, in ICU, a clock moved backward, and now, I couldn't see the one in here. How frustrating! I didn't know why knowing the time was so important, but it was.

Before I had been released from ICU, I had talked to my sister, Sue, on the phone, and she had told me the dreams I had been experiencing were not something to be concerned about.

"Don't worry about it," she said, "Opiates will do that."

Opiates?? What opiates? "How did you become an expert?" I asked her.

I heard her chuckle. "Think back to the sixties," she said. "I have a bit of a history." Sue had been a "wild-child" when we were both a lot younger. She had been the only one who could get away with doing what she wanted. I guess, since she was the youngest, our dad either gave up or she had him wrapped around her finger. Your guess is as good as mine. But she had more

Paul Haber

than a passing acquaintance with "recreational" drugs back then.

CHAPTER 18
BABY SISTERS ARE A GIFT

Of course, we knew Mom was going to have another baby, so when school was out for the summer, and Dad took us down to Pennsylvania to visit my aunt and uncle, we began to celebrate.

Mary Beth and Pete, my sister and brother, were only four and two years old, respectively, and they were much more excited about the new baby than I was. While I was happy, I was eleven years old now and much too cool to get fired up about a mere baby. Besides, I already had a couple of those.

But, when we got home a week or so later, and I got a chance to hold my new sister, Suzanna Lynne- Suzie, from the first day, all that coolness went away. She was a chubby little angel, who, as she grew a little older, showed the uncanny ability to wrap Dad around her little finger. She got away with childish stuff that we

Paul Haber

would've been punished for. It wasn't just Dad, though; she could maneuver her oldest brother pretty well too.

Since there were few children in the immediate area, the Haber kids played among themselves with big brother Paul as the ringleader.

One winter morning, probably on a Saturday since we weren't in school, Mom got up to a quiet house. Instantly suspicious, she went into the girls' room to check on them only to find empty beds. The room I shared with my brother, Pete, was next and also empty, but the window was open—interior pane, the storm window, and the screen on the outside.

Mom looked out the window to see footprints in the snow drift outside our house. We lived in western New York and got the full Lake Effect with weather coming off Lakes Erie and Ontario. That meant lots and lots of snow during the winter followed by ice storms in February and March. The snow was usually so deep that Dad would park out by the road rather than trying to keep the hundred or so foot-long driveway clear. The snowblower didn't come to our house until after I left for the Marines.

Mom was not enthused that I had lowered my brother and two sisters out of the bedroom window and led them through the snow to who knows where. The weather was

Chronicles of A Blessed Man

especially bitter that day with lots of wind, blowing snow, and frigid temperatures. Needless to say, when we finally returned, Mom was waiting for us with fire in her eyes.

But, Hallelujah! Everybody was fine—rosy-cheeked and laughing even Suzie, who we pulled through the snow on a sled. The snow was taller than she was in places.

When she hit her teen years in the sixties, she got into the usual—boys, pot, and all the rest. She managed to survive the period, but I thought she'd finally gone crazy when she hooked up with Hal Goddard, a man almost her father's age.

What did I know? They were almost unreasonably happy for years until he passed away from emphysema but not before blessing her with two children, Rachel and Adam. Hal had made his living as a pilot and flying instructor. He had done some "Black Ops" for the government, and we talked several times, trying to determine if he had been the pilot on any of my missions. If the speeches at his memorial were any indication, he was some hot-shot in the air. I only flew with him once that I'm sure of. That was in an aerobatics airplane, and he made that thing do everything but talk. He scared the tar out of me!

Paul Haber

A few years after Hal's death, Suzie, okay, okay, by then it was Sue, met Brent Baber, a musician and aircraft mechanic. He must've been good at his job because he was paid crazy sums to move to Reno, Nevada, to work there. They had returned a few months before.

Brent and Suzie married, and Sue became step-mom to Brent's adult children. Our clan understands blended families for certain.

When they heard I was in the hospital and in a normal ward, they quickly brought me a laptop computer, so I could keep track of by business. Most importantly, they said I had to write about my experience. So, I guess you could blame Sue and Brent for this book. I'll always be grateful!

I don't know whether it was the residual drugs in my system or Sue planting a suggestion in my head, but when I finally went back to sleep, I had a new set of dreams. Now I was "flying" through the most blasted, dirty, depressing country I had ever seen. The flat desert floor was filled with some sort of sickly green plants that looked like diseased aloe Vera or agave plants. They were huge, and their leaves were being constantly blown about by what looked like small tornados or large dust devils that sprouted up everywhere.

Chronicles of A Blessed Man

I say I was flying because I didn't seem to be using my legs, but I was moving at a high rate of speed over the endless landscape. I was having trouble dodging the whirlwinds. It seemed as if they were chasing me, and there were so many!

I woke up and moved my head to the right slightly as if that would change the dream. It worked. Now, I was in a small room surrounded by what appeared to be a Mexican family—Mom, Dad, and several very cute youngsters who all looked as if they were under five. I had no idea what I was doing there, but the kids seemed to know me as they called me Viejo—the old one. They acted as if I were their grandfather or some sort of respected elder.

I woke up suddenly. I didn't want to be somebody's Viejo. I wanted to be me, back home, back with my exercise equipment, and karate classes.

I was so tired, exhausted, and drifted back to sleep—back into the desert with the whirlwinds and the plants. I jerked awake only to drift back out into the Mexican room again. I don't know how many times I switched from flying over the desert to being in that little room. I was beginning to panic. It was as if the desert were on a screen on the left side of the hospital room and the little room with the kids was in the center. That gave me an idea. I turned my head to my right to a blank space and visualized Kyehwa. I did a type of meditation, focusing on her smiling face. It took some effort. As I would start to drift off to sleep, I'd go back to the two places I didn't want to be. When that happened, I would "change the channel" and get back to my bride. I dropped off to sleep for about four hours.

Wednesday began with the bustle of shift change. Another pair of stunning young ladies, always cheerful and very, very courteous, came on shift, a nurse and a med tech as usual. Vitals were taken, I was once again asked my full name and date of birth, in order to verify that the meds were being given to the correct patient. Someone hung a new bottle of simple saline and another bag of the "milkshake," liquid nutrition with, I believe, two or three thousand calories per bag. About two bags a day were running through the IV, which came to me through a tube inserted into the Vena Cava, the large vein near my heart.

I had nothing to do. I didn't have my glasses or anything to read even if I could see. The television was off, and the curtains were open. There was a kind of night light but nothing bright enough to read. At least, I could now make out the clock on the wall. 7:30 AM. My bed was by the window, and there was some light

Chronicles of A Blessed Man

coming through-enough to tell it was morning. Somehow, it helped to know what time of day it was.

The tech brought my breakfast, a fresh cup of ice chips. Yum, yum. I got two small cups per shift, six in 24 hours. I asked if there was any chance I could get some food, but she said not for a day or so. I would continue to get my nutrition through the IV for a while. That figured since the surgery had been on my intestines, and I wasn't hungry anyway. But it would have been nice to have a real drink- even water.

A little later about 8:15, a lady from physical therapy came to visit and to make me walk with a walker. I wasn't too sure about that but was game to try, so I sat up too quickly, I guess. She told me not to use my stomach muscles. Too late! Then, as directed, I swung my legs over the side of the bed and slid toward the edge.

"Do you need some help?" she asked.

"I don't know. I think I've got it," I answered. I got my feet under me and did the top half of a squat exercise, carefully getting my weight balanced over my feet. "Piece of cake," I grunted.

She showed me how to position the walker, with my IV tree, and said that I should take one step at a time. Yeah, right! That lasted until I got past the door of the room. Then it was "let's go for a stroll time." I moved out as quickly as I could with that piece of aluminum in front of me and the IV tree dragging by the other hand. The PT rep was impressed. We went about forty feet down the hall, turned slowly, and back. When we arrived at my room, she told me to go on in, and she helped me maneuver the walker to my bed. Now, that was a day's work!

"That's enough for now," she said.

Thank God, I thought. I could try to act like a hero, but man, that was tough! Time for a break.

After helping me back in bed, she told me I should walk as many times a day as I could, no less than then 10 minutes per day. That brought back memories of the last time I had experienced surgery a few years earlier. The nurse had told me to walk then too. I did- I took off and walked laps for forty minutes. Somehow, though, I didn't think I was quite ready for that this time.

She also told me she was leaving the walker, so I could use it. I never did. I just held on to the IV tree for whatever balance help I needed. I didn't feel like I had enough hands to maneuver the walker and IV at the same time. I managed at least one more walk around the ward that day and two or three every other day I was in the hospital, some of them a half-hour long. Nothing like being a type-A personality!

It was a pain to have to bother the staff to unplug the electrical cord to the IV every couple of hours for my walk, so after a couple of days, I did it myself. When I told the nurse, she said, "Oh, okay! No problem?"

"Piece of cake," I responded. That was becoming my favorite phrase.

I had called home earlier that morning, waking up everybody after they had only been asleep a few hours. I wanted to let them know what room I was in. I found out they had been advised the night before. Oh, well. Nobody tells me anything. I'm only the patient.

About ten o'clock, Kyehwa and Ronnie came in, and I told them about the crazy dreams. They filled me in on what had been happening "outside" and tried again to make me understand just what had been going on with me and how long it had been. Kyehwa kept fussing with my hair, scratching my arm and so on, and after a while, I griped about it, not realizing that was how she had maintained a connection with me when I was unconscious. It was very important to her, and I guess I hurt her feelings because she turned her back and seemed to be quite angry. I couldn't imagine why. They left shortly after to take Ronnie to the airport, and Kyehwa didn't return until the next day. Bummer!

Sometime in the late morning or early afternoon, as the day was still dragging, I was still dozing, and my roommate was still hanging around. I got visitors. Our neighbor and friend Linda Cornett along with Andrea Horney, and Jane Akers, other friends from our weekly Bible study arrived to cheer up the "sick guy." I was sitting up in bed, grateful for the company, and we had a great gab-fest.

During the conversation, I made the comment that since God had allowed me to come back from what everybody told me was near-death, I guessed I would have to become nicer. My wise-girl neighbor, Jane, smiled and said, "Can we get that in writing?"

"Absolutely," I responded. "Anybody got paper and pen?" Those items were soon handed to me and I wrote. "NICE-ER."

"I didn't promise to be nice all the time," I told them, "just nice-er!" That brought a chuckle and the usual disparaging comments I could expect from that trio.

After a little while, Jane found a blue vinyl glove, the type that was used by staff for non-sterile situations such as cleaning up, etc. I saw her blow it up like a balloon, then she found a marker and scribbled something on the

Chronicles of A Blessed Man

inflated glove. A moment later, she presented me with the glove with a happy face drawn on it.

"What am I going to do with that?" I asked.

"I made you a punching bag." Jane smiled.

Now that made sense to me! In a few minutes, we had figured out how to tie it to a piece of string, which I disconnected from one of the lights in my area, and we tied the glove over my head where I could play with it like a boxer hitting a speed bag. Simple minds have simple pleasures, I guess. That thing stayed there and was punched on until I left the hospital several days later. Thanks, Jane! You helped keep me sane for six days.

CHAPTER 19
NEVER A PLAIN JANE

Jane was one of the folks I met through the Cornetts and their Bible study. She and her husband, Joe, were regulars at the Tuesday meeting and had become great friends.

Jane was an Army brat, and like most of that breed, her family had lived all over the world. But they settled in Warminster, Pennsylvania, when Jane was five. When she was thirteen, she met Joe. They lived on the same street and attended the same school. When they started dating, their big dates were at the local Laundromat! There were only about three thousand residents in the whole township, a part of Bucks County. It wasn't easy finding exciting things to do, but they managed.

In time, they married and had four kids, "two each" as Jane says, and they moved to Arizona somewhere along the way where Joe worked for the local electrical cooperative as a supervisor. Along with working at the

Chronicles of A Blessed Man

local school for fourteen years, Jane was grandmother to five grandchildren. I guess that's where she learned her wry sense of humor. How did I find such great friends?

After Jane, Linda, and Andrea went home, "sister Sue" and her better half, Brent, showed up with the laptop computer they loaned me to use while I was stuck in the hospital. Great! Now, I could check my e-mail and catch up on what was going on in our business, even the news . It also gave me the idea for these Chronicles, so, as I said earlier, you can all blame Sue and Brent.

I was realizing at that point how fortunate I really was to have such great friends and relatives, who cared enough to travel. None of them lived closed to St. Joseph's Hospital, and some were from forty miles away. They still brought me, or in Jane's case manufactured, gifts and such. I am truly blessed. Hence, the title of this rambling missive. What I didn't realize at the time was that this was only the beginning of a strange and wonderful turn in my life.

Sue and Brent stayed an hour or so, and somewhere along the way, I think Sandra Perfetto showed up. Things have become kind of run together as far as what happened on which day. I'm pretty sure it was Wednesday that Sandra came, and I think both she and her husband Mike came back the next day. I could be wrong about that, but I saw a lot of Sandra while I was "incarcerated." As I said, good friends!

The day passed much quicker thanks to all the visitors, and I barely noticed my roommate finally get released during the afternoon sometime. For a while, I had the whole room to myself.

The visitors weren't done though. Dave Parker, a fellow martial-arts "educator," Shihan, and the guy I go to when I have a question about martial arts history, arrived with his delightful wife, Ruth and a couple of books around five in the evening. I call Dave my "Brother of the Spear" because of our mutual passion for all things martial especially Okinawan.

Chronicles of A Blessed Man

CHAPTER 20
SENSEI DAVE

I met Dave Parker in 1996 when I was introduced to the Martial Arts organization called Kodenkan Yudanshakai, Institute of the Ancient Arts Black Belt Society. His attitude, humor, and exceptional skill as a martial artist and teacher made our early friendship an easy fit.

Dave had been born in Sacramento, California, in 1954, which made him eight years younger than I, but his knowledge of the history of the Japanese martial arts is exemplary. I began learning from him almost as soon as we met.

He had lived in Hawaii from 1960 to 1970 and studied Danzan-ryu jujutsu in 1966 and 1967 but didn't begin studying Karate until 1970 when he lived in Oregon.

After his family moved to Tucson, Arizona, Dave began training under Sensei Barry Holck at the Ott

Paul Haber

Family YMCA. The Holck family were Japanese-Hawaiians who had become near legends in Judo, Danzan-ryu and other martial arts in Arizona. The patriarch of the clan was Joe Holck, born Joshiro Matsuno, who was a cultural icon among martial artists by the time I met him. Joe had studied Jujutsu, Judo, karate, and several other arts, and for years, dominated the Judo scene in the American southwest. He was also one of the five founders of an eclectic martial art called Kajukenbo. Barry was also trained in several arts but specialized in Shorin-ryu Karate, a classical Okinawan style. Dave studied karate with Barry and Danzan-ryu under Joe, both at the "Y."

His training at the Ott "Y" was an extremely fortunate occurrence for Dave as he met the love of his life there. Ruth worked at the front desk, and Dave says he would make special trips to the water fountain, "just to go see the babe at the front desk." They married in 1985 and raised three sons. Two of them were studying when I joined the Yudanshakai.

Ruthie and Dave seemed the perfect pair, friendly, humorous, and especially Ruthie, loving. I never met her without getting a hug and usually a kiss on the cheek. Ruth didn't study the martial arts, but her life with Dave, coupled with a long and successful career as a Physical

Chronicles of A Blessed Man

Education teacher, made her the "go-to" whenever we organized a tournament or ceremony. But most important of all, they were my friends.

I got a kiss from Ruthie, a handshake from Dave, and could barely contain myself not to look at the books while we chatted. Dave knows what I like and always brings just the right book. And he came through again. He brought two books that absolutely fascinated me, and one of them was about the Japanese master I had studied under more than forty years before. I was enthralled.

Ruthie is used to martial-arts-crazy people, so she was very patient with us, but I worked hard to let her know how much I appreciated her coming. Dave already knew how I felt, I think. They stayed an hour or so and left me to watch some drivel on television. I didn't have my glasses, so I couldn't read the books until the next day. Kyehwa had said she would bring the glasses and hearing aids when she came on Thursday.

About ten or eleven, I tried to settle off to sleep. What happened then is the next chapter—and a whole other story!

CHAPTER 21
THE HOWLER IN THE NIGHT

As I lay in bed, surrounded by at least a half-dozen pillows, I dreaded going to sleep. What if those dreams returned? Maybe, it was caused by the residual drugs in my system, and maybe, they were gone now…or maybe not.

I thought of a conversation I had with Linda Cornett earlier in the day about the previous Friday while I was still in an induced coma, recovering from the second surgery. According to the story, it was a stormy night with rain and lightning as usual during the Arizona monsoons in August. It fit the mood in the neighborhood especially at our house. Kyehwa was exhausted, I had just gone through the second surgery and was still unconscious. I would be for another two and a half days, but nobody knew that then.

Chronicles of A Blessed Man

The rain was pouring down, but Kyehwa and the visitors were safe at home when Linda looked out across the street to my house. What she saw shocked her. Arching directly over the Haber home were not one but two complete rainbows!

Now, think about that. How many times have you even seen one complete rainbow? You know, the arch and both ends? This time, she could see both ends of two complete rainbows, and my house was centered under both of them.

As she told me this story, I must admit that I was slightly skeptical. I tried to act as if I was buying the whole story as outlandish as it was. Then she pulled out her cell phone, and there was a picture of Kyehwa in front of our house and two rainbows. Jane, who lived in the opposite direction, told me that she, too, had seen the unusual (miraculous?) sight even though the light should have been coming from the other direction. How was that possible?

The consensus was that God was telling everyone that all was okay. He had it under control, and they shouldn't worry. Linda said it convinced her; I don't know about Kyehwa. As I thought about it that Wednesday night, I mused that it was no stranger than everything that had happened to me in the past week (?), several days, anyway. As I began to piece everything together, I realized that if both my vehicles had not needed repair at the same time, if the parts had been more readily available, or if I had departed on the road trip to Ontario, California, that morning as scheduled when I collapsed, I would have been somewhere in the desert, west of Phoenix and who knows how far from a hospital. I got a chill, lying there in the hospital bed. The Lord had definitely intervened in my life this time. I had no doubt. Why? What was it all about?

Why had I been rescued? Apparently, I still had something important to accomplish, but what? Kyehwa and I had a business that we'd been working at off and on for several years. The potential, both for income and for helping people, were outstanding, but we really hadn't put as much effort into it as we should. Could that be it?

I had been teaching martial arts for over thirty years and absolutely loved it, but could that be the important mission? It's true that I could help people in several ways, self-defense of course, increasing their self-esteem, and improving their fitness level. Was that important enough?

I had been stressing about the way my teaching and personal improvement had been going and contemplating making some changes in how and what I taught. But I still hadn't been able to pin down specifics. Likewise, since the Gastric Bypass two years before, I had been working hard on fitness and learning more about how to coach others, starting from their present level rather than trying to push them ahead of their capacity. My initial training in the military didn't prepare me to work with non-military people, those "soft civilians."

Then, there was my Christian walk. I had been saved years before, after going about as far to the "Dark Side" as any man could go and still survive. I had spent years seeking forgiveness from those I had injured, and I guess I'd made some progress, but could that be what I needed to do for God?

Kyehwa and I had quickly agreed to join a Bible study with Larry and Linda Cornett shortly after we had moved into our home, and that was enjoyable. I had read enough previously that I could understand most of what we were studying. In fact, when Larry posed a question, I tended to jump in with an answer. Linda finally put me on a five-second (later expanded to 10) count before I was allowed to answer, just to give the rest of the group a chance. It wasn't that I was more knowledgeable but

Paul Haber

just more outspoken. Maybe I needed to grow more in that area.

I spent several hours in that hospital bed, going in circles over all those question but found no answers.

Earlier, when the night shift came on, I found that not everyone working in the ward was a pretty young girl. As I dozed about 7:30 pm, a deep voice woke me, saying, "Hi! My name's Paul, and I'm your tech this evening." I opened my eyes to see a good-looking guy, probably in his thirties, dressed in the scrubs that all the staff wore. But he was definitely not a young woman. So much for that theory! In later conversations, I found he was a Mexican-Japanese native of Tucson-I told him I didn't believe there was any such thing- and that he said he had been one of the first graduates of the Medical Technician program in Tucson. He seemed a very sharp guy.

We had talked for a few minutes, then he told me about Elizabeth, the nurse who would be covering my room. He had returned several times to take vitals, etc.

Paul had told me that Elizabeth sometimes "put people off" because of her voice. Patients sometimes mistook her natural tone for anger. I had thanked him for the tip and was prepared to be patient with this nurse

Chronicles of A Blessed Man

when she finally made an appearance. She was covering several rooms and didn't come in for a while.

I was dozing again, when I heard a soft, musical voice say, "Mister Haber, I have your meds. Can you tell me your full name and date of birth?"

I opened my eyes to see a cheerful, reasonably attractive lady with a moon-shaped face so black it was almost blue. I had been told she was from Nigeria, but this wasn't the voice I had been expecting. I answered her question, I was getting pretty good at it by now, and she went about giving me a couple of injections and adding some more bags to my IV set-up. We talked briefly, and I decided that if her voice sounded harsh to someone, they must have very sensitive ears. I found her voice a pleasure to listen to.

As I finally got my mind clear enough to try to sleep, I decided that I was going to try to sleep on my side, as I did at home, without asking anyone's advice. I fussed and moved, arranging the bed and all within to my satisfaction. it took quite a while, but I finally got to sleep on my left side.

A little while later, I heard Elizabeth's voice softly ask, "Mister Haber, why are you lying like that?"

Paul Haber

I told her I wanted to sleep on my side, and I heard her sigh, "We do not recommend sleeping like that," she said. "Your tubes are all twisted."

I realized then that the beeping sound that I had been hearing had been the IV machine, complaining the tubes were crimped. It took over an hour of Elizabeth's patient work to sort it all out. Somehow, tape that was holding tubes to my body had disconnected and stuck itself to the sheets and blanket. What a mess! Before she left, Elizabeth made me give her my word that I would remain on my back. I did and finally dozed off.

Sometime in the night, the screen was closed between my bed and the clock, I was awakened by the most hideous cry I had ever heard. I sounded like a cross between a wolf's howl and what I imagined a banshee would sound like. It jolted me so much that I sat up in bed without use of hands, which is not recommended after abdominal surgery, and looked around wildly. I knew I didn't have a roommate yet. No one had moved in since the previous afternoon, but what was that sound?

There it was again. Finally, I recognized it as a human voice in pain. Just for a moment, I reverted to my old attitude.

Chronicles of A Blessed Man

"Good Lord, dude, grow a pair, will you?" I grunted. Then I remembered. I was supposed to be a nice-er guy these days. I had given the promise in writing after all. I settled back into my bed and spent a few moments praying.

"Lord, if it be your will, help that poor soul. Give him relief from whatever is causing the pain. Give him healing or relief as you will, Lord, but please don't make him suffer so much."

As if my prayer had helped me as well, and hopefully, whoever was howling, I soon dropped off to sleep for about five hours, which was the longest "nap" I had had since waking up in ICU on Monday night.

I woke up when Paul came back in to give me one final check before going off shift. We talked about how his parents had managed to get together, an Arizona-born Mexican in the U.S. Navy who found his bride in Japan and brought her back to Tucson. It was a pretty interesting story, and he was a very friendly young man who was a great comfort to my still confused mind.

As he was preparing to leave, I asked, "Paul, did you hear that unearthly howling during the night? What was that?"

His face took on a look of pity. "That's an elderly lady down the hall," he said. "She's completely eaten up with cancer, and there's nothing they can do for her except try to make it easier. Any time they touch her to roll her over or change her gown, the pain is so great, she screams like that."

I was speechless. After Paul left the room, I said a prayer of thanks that I had remembered to change my attitude to one of pity earlier in the night. I would have felt terrible if I had maintained the old tough-guy attitude. That poor old lady. She remained in my thoughts the rest of the day. Maybe I could make other changes too.

CHAPTER 22
THE ROAD TO DAMASCUS

Thursday began as always at St. Joseph's Hospital—first a stirring, a rustle, then footsteps, squeaking wheels of carts for medicine, blood and all the other stuff they used, finally, voices, announcements on the speaker system, and the sound of televisions going on. Just a normal day.

Since I was still on ice chips and the bag of "milkshake" hanging on the IV tree, there was no breakfast to enjoy, but at least, I didn't have a roommate eating breakfast while I went without. While I still wasn't hungry, the smell of food going past my room was enticing, too much so.

The new day shift came on, meds were changed, and when the tech came in, I asked if she could unplug the IV tree from the electric plug so that I could take my first walk of the day. Dr. Wang, the "pulmonary dude," had ordered me to walk at least twice a day and to use the breathing device, he called it the "blowing machine", every waking hour. I had been faithful to the machine and was looking forward to walking a bit just to get out of bed.

She unplugged the IV, wrapped the cord around the box, and asked if I needed help getting out of bed.

"Could you just stand by for a second?" I asked. "I think I can handle it, but we'll see."

I carefully placed my feet on the floor, clad in the cutesy blue socks provided by the hospital. Yesterday, I had been wearing yellow socks Kyehwa had put on in ICU, which were worn by those not authorized to walk around by themselves. Later in the afternoon on Wednesday, they had been exchanged for the blue—my ticket to walk. After a long, slow breath, I slid my weight over my feet, and I was erect. No problem. I smiled at the tech, got a good grip on the rolling IV tree, and maneuvered the thing past the bed and out into the corridor.

Free at last! It had been about sixty hours since I woke up in ICU (things like that weigh heavy on your mind when you're stuck in bed), and it was a real joy to make my way slowly down the hall toward the nurse's station then to "unknown territory" at the other end of

Chronicles of A Blessed Man

the ward. I went past the lounge where the nurses went to complete their paperwork, took a right past some offices, and down another hall to what looked like a waiting room complete with leather couches and easy chairs. Another right took me to yet another corridor then back to the nurse's station.

Okay! That was about the extent of the scenery, I guess. At the main hallway, I took a left and headed past my room to the end of the hallway that marked by closed swinging doors. I did a slow u turn, and my balance felt fine, but have you ever tried to do a "yooie" with an IV tree? Not the most convenient thing to drag with you. I didn't care. I did two or three more laps from one end of the ward to the other and finally realized that I was getting tired…quite tired and very suddenly.

I wandered back to my bed, maneuvered the IV tree back into place, and lay down with a sigh. After I got the blankets, IV tubes and me all squared away, I pushed the button for the nurse, so someone could plug the IV back in.

By the time someone responded, which was probably two minutes, I was already asleep and woke up immediately when the tech came into the room. I realized that my sleep pattern was messed up, and if I didn't do something about it deliberately, it would remain so. I would just have to "bite the bullet" and stay awake during the day, so I could sleep at night.

Sometime that morning, my new "roomie" arrived. I couldn't see him because of the screen, but his voice sounded pretty bad. He breathed with a wheeze and seemed to whine a lot. He was already giving the staff a hard time, and I heaved a large sigh. So much for peace and quiet.

His name, I heard, was Robert, and judging by his voice, I figured he was in his seventies or so. I was quite surprised the next day when I was told he was ninety-two. Robert was a pretty sick man as I heard when I eavesdropped on his conversation with Dr. Wang. Actually, the doc conducted a monologue. I heard that Robert was suffering from pneumonia, had not been using his breathing apparatus (the blowing machine) as he had been told, and had taken a turn for the worse as a result.

I was impressed with the husky Dr. Wang, as he managed to chew Robert's butt very completely without being rude or disrespectful. He told Robert that if he ever wanted to get out of the hospital and go home, he needed to follow the instructions, do his breathing exercises, and cooperate with the hospital staff.

Chronicles of A Blessed Man

Wang finally ended his lecture with several encouraging comments. "You can do it!" He left. Robert was quiet for only a few minutes before he began shouting.

"Help me!" he wheezed. "Can somebody help me?"

The nurse must have been nearby as she arrived in only a few seconds. "How can I help you?" she asked.

"My arm is stuck," Robert replied.

The nurse fussed with pillows and Robert's arm, trying to make him comfortable, but he was not satisfied.

"Can you make the bed flatter? My neck is crooked." On and on, his complaints continued.

The nurse or tech would hardly be out of the room when Robert would start shouting for help. He couldn't find his water pitcher, his back was crooked in the bed, he had to go to the bathroom, he wasn't allowed out of bed since he was too weak to stand, and on and on. I don't think he was quiet for an hour at any one time. I was very aggravated but kept my big trap shut for once. I just wish he would listen to the staff and push the call button for the nurse instead of shouting like he was dying. Good grief!

Kyehwa came in around 10:30, and we sat and talked. Somebody had come and removed the gastro-nasal bypass earlier that morning, so I could talk a little better, but my voice was still raspy and hoarse from being irritated by the tube I had been wearing since I woke up in ICU.

At least, I didn't have that blasted stick protruding from my nose anymore. Kyehwa had also brought my glasses and hearing aids along with a couple of my books. Now, I could pass the time, reading. Without the glasses, even the television was blurry enough to give me a headache. This was much better!

We were having a relatively quiet morning except for Robert until Kyehwa's normal generous nature got her into a situation. Robert was crying out for someone to come and fix his pillows because his neck was crooked, and Kyehwa went to his rescue. Big mistake! For the rest of her visit, Robert kept calling her to help him.

"Lady, can you help me?"

It is, of course, against the rules. She quickly learned to ignore him. It wasn't easy, but we went on with our visit.

Around noon, another friend, Mike Perfetto, arrived from Wilcox, some hundred miles away, and Kyehwa left to take care of errands while Mike accompanied me on another walk. We slowly circumnavigated the ward a few times, talking about guns, which we both enjoy as well as catching up on the latest "gossip" in the

Chronicles of A Blessed Man

Department of Corrections where I had worked until June and Mike still worked. His wife, Sandra, had "pulled the plug" and left the department some time before in protest over policy changes she felt, correctly, were not only foolish but were dangerous.

I knew the word had gone around the department about my situation since I had received calls and reports of calls from people I had worked with and some I had not seen in years. I was kind of humbled. I didn't know that many people remembered me or that they cared enough to call. Wow!

Mike's wife, Sandra, arrived in the afternoon and stayed for a while, and I read for a while. My eyes seemed to get tired very quickly, so I ended up watching the TV for a while.

Lunch was a treat, liquid diet! It wasn't much, but it sure beat ice chips! The rumor was that if I did okay with the liquid, I could move on to something more substantial. I was still attached to the "milkshake,' but that, too, would change that evening if all went well. I was confident, other than the obvious, the hernia in my intestine, I was known for having a "cast-iron" stomach. No food bothered me much, so with a little luck, maybe I could get on real food in a day or so.

Paul Haber

While I was waiting for dinner, my friend Josh Parker arrived. Josh was the son of Dave and Ruth, who had visited the day before. Another martial artist, Josh and I had known each other since he was a young teenager and we had always enjoyed each other's company. Of course, our primary conversation was about the martial arts like karate, Jujutsu, and so forth, but that was just fine with me.

Josh filled me in on what was going on in our little world of martial arts "freaks," and we discussed some of the things that had been on my mind about that subject, changes I was considering, and was not sure how to implement. He also told me his folks were planning on returning to visit on Saturday on their way back from Mexico. He said I should talk to his dad about my uncertainty. Good idea! Dave was someone I could always depend on for good advice.

After an hour or so, Josh departed and I was alone again except for Robert, who had been sleeping for a couple of hours and chose now to wake up.

After dinner, as the ward began to settle down for the night, I forced myself to stay awake until about nine o'clock. Then I drifted off, hoping I could sleep for several hours. No way!

Chronicles of A Blessed Man

Between Robert acting out and just being restless, I was awake every hour until about one in the morning. I woke up and just could not drop back off. I fretted, tried to meditate, and counted sheep. I did everything I knew to try to get some sleep. Finally, about two o'clock, my frustration finally got the best of me.

"God,'" I prayed, "Please let me sleep! I need to sleep!"

A soft voice spoke in my ear, "You don't need to sleep. You need to plan." I know this sounds like a hallucination, but I know it was real. I heard the voice as clearly as anything I had ever heard, and I knew whose Voice it was—a still quiet voice I had only heard about in the Bible. I sat bolt upright in my bed and looked around. There was no one there, of course. I guess I was expecting a burning bush or something, but no such luck.

I immediately settled back into the bed as my mind was going a mile a minute. As soon as I gave up trying to sleep, I was awake and alert and suddenly knew the answer to all the things that had been bothering me.

For the past several months, I had felt guilty about "wasting" my time teaching and practicing the martial arts because it took time away from more important things like my relationship with my wife. Also, always in need of improvement was our business, which was paying a small amount of money regularly but with potential I hadn't begun to tap, the "honey-do" list around our home, some of which had been waiting almost two years. Then there was my duty to my God, to spread the word of salvation. Even though I was retired, I was unable to give each the time they needed and could not bring myself to do what I thought was necessary, to stop "wasting" time on the relatively unimportant tasks like Karate, which I loved, and get serious about building a legacy for my wife and descendants, and at the same time, help others to know God.

As I lay there on Thursday night, suddenly everything became clear. The martial arts, the chores, the time with Kyehwa, and the business were not all different roads, ach leading to its own destination. They were all part of the same destiny! They were all methods to help other people escape their fear!

With the martial arts and fitness training, I could help them develop an attitude of personal safety and health and increase self-esteem in the process. With the multi-level business and the people skills I had learned and was continuing to learn, I could help people escape their fear of poverty, pay off their bills, begin to save for the future, and develop financial security for them and their

Chronicles of A Blessed Man

families. With both of these, as I was helping others in the short run, I was gaining influence, which, if I was careful and put their needs first, could lead them to Christ.

Several times in the past, I had experienced the intense joy when I had sponsored someone into our business, taken them to a major conference, and seen them go forward during the altar call, which was held at the voluntary non-denominational service offered on Sunday.

These different things I had been doing were not different roads at all. They were all lanes on the same super highway to Jesus. My heart was pounding. Sleep was not even an issue anymore. I knew what I had to do! I spent a couple of hours thinking about the details on how I could implement what I had just learned.

I got a vision, there in the dark, of Saul of Tarsus being knocked from his horse by a bright light. Well, I had sure been knocked off my high horse in the past couple of weeks too. Maybe this was my road to Damascus.

I slept soundly the rest of that night.

CHAPTER 23
A CHANGE OF ATTITUDE

That is…I slept soundly until good old Robert, the roommate, started acting up. He was apparently in pain, couldn't move enough in the bed to get comfortable, and didn't understand that he was not the only patient on the floor. He also couldn't seem to find the call button, so he would cry out in a voice surprising strong for a man with pneumonia.

"Help me! Won't somebody help me!" he cried over and over. It seemed every five minutes that a nurse or tech rushed into the room, trying to shush him. Paul, the med tech, finally sat down with Robert and explained that Robert was not allowed to get out of bed because he was too weak to walk. He had already tried to negotiate his way to the toilet twice and had fallen both times. If he needed to go to the bathroom, he would have to use the bedpan, which Robert refused to do.

Chronicles of A Blessed Man

Paul explained very patiently, I thought, that if Robert continued to put himself at risk, the staff would secure him to the bed with straps. The doctor had already given permission for them to do so in order to protect him from his own foolishness.

Around five or six in the morning, permission finally came from Robert's physician to give him a mild sedative. Ten minutes after the needle went in, Robert was asleep. I wasn't far behind.

I woke up again when Paul came back in just before seven for one last set of vitals. As we chatted, I told him that I had been seriously considering having a "come to Jesus meeting" with Robert if he had not finally gone to sleep. Paul only commented that some patients needed more attention than others, and that's what made his job more difficult. He also told me that Robert, when he was not a patient, actually was a volunteer in the same hospital. He pushed wheelchairs, and so on, for other patients.

Robert lived in a Senior Center. His daughter, who the hospital had managed to contact to get permission to treat him and necessary insurance information, lived in El Paso, Texas, and Robert didn't see her very much. She was on her way to Tucson on Friday to sign paperwork and visit her ill father. Maybe it would help. I hoped so.

I dozed, read, and watched some television until Kyehwa arrived about ten-thirty. Then I dragged my sleepy body out of bed for a walk with Kyehwa on one side and the IV tree on the other. The Charge Nurse on the ward had given me permission to unplug and re-plug my own tree rather than wait for a staff member to have a free moment. This had, of course, came about after I had gone ahead and done it several times anyway, and with no dizziness or other ill effects, I walked to her station and told her what I had done. It saved everybody a bit of work, and I could come and go as I pleased. After all, the doctors wanted me to walk, didn't they?

The toughest part of the whole deal was getting the tree past my bed and into the hallway. After that, it was a piece of cake!

Kyehwa stayed a few hours and went home to catch up on her sleep. The night before, after she had come in early to the hospital and spent several hours with me, she had driven to Phoenix, about two hours, to a skin care seminar with our daughter Marina and Jonnie Couillard, who had recently joined our business. She had returned home well after midnight but had risen early again just

Chronicles of A Blessed Man

to visit me. It made me feel kind of guilty and very appreciative.

I had been put on a liquid diet the previous noon, and for breakfast, was advanced to full liquids. I got Jell-O, yogurt, and the like. Yahoo! Since I tolerated it well, for Lunch, I moved up to soft foods like oatmeal, etc. I got plenty of juice, milk, and Praise the Lord, coffee. I think I missed coffee more than the food.

A couple of hours after lunch, I was visited by one of my doctors, Dr. Song. I had three physicians, counting the surgeon, Dr. Harmon, the pulmonary specialist, Dr. Wang, and Song, who acted as Primary Care for all the hospital patients. Dr. Song told me that they had been considering sending me home on Saturday, but he was not recommending it since my white blood count was slightly elevated.

"It's only slightly elevated," he told me, "but it's better to find out what's causing it and treat it here rather than you have a relapse and have to come back to the hospital."

"Yeah," I agreed. "I'll vote for that. I can put up with another day or two."

Song told me that he had scheduled a CAT scan for later that day just to look for any infection in my bowels. He told me that I had had one previously before the surgery, but, of course, I didn't remember anything about it. He also gave me some good news. He was putting me on a regular diet for dinner.

Talk about fast! In four meals, I had gone from ice chips to regular food. As he left, I was wondering what dinner would bring. I found out only a few minutes later when the woman who took orders for the kitchen came in and gave me a list of possibilities. She got as far as sirloin steak and I said, "Stop! That's all I need to hear. I'll have steak."

I finally went up for the CAT scan about three-thirty and got back to my bed about five, only minutes before my dinner arrived. Talk about a Hallelujah breakdown! A steak, O'Brien potatoes, a dinner roll, and mixed vegetables. Yes, I was looking forward to real food.

I was smart enough to know that I couldn't finish it all, but it was tempting! I worked my way through the beef and most of the potatoes, leaving only a little of the rest. I moved the dessert to the side to tackle that later!

I topped it off with coffee as I leaned back on the bed, which was raised to a sitting position. What a life! I felt as if I were King of the World. Only a week prior, I had been in a coma. The rest of the day went quietly until Mike Reynolds came to visit after he had taught our Karate class.

Chronicles of A Blessed Man

Mike lived about thirteen miles off the interstate on a hundred acres of desert about thirty-five or forty miles from Tucson. Of course, his way home was opposite the direction to St. Joseph's, but he came anyway. I was beginning to see a pattern. There were a lot of people willing to put themselves out for me with visits and phone calls, the laptop my sister and brother-in-law had lent me, cards, letters and on and on.

I wasn't used to feeling humble. Anyone who knows me, knows I tend to be just a tad cocky, maybe even arrogant at times, but wow! As Mike left after talking about martial arts for an hour or so, I actually had tears in my eyes. What did I do to deserve such good friends? Maybe I really did need to be a "nice-er" guy as I had told my friends on Wednesday.

I also noticed that the room was much quieter this day. Robert had gone somewhere to receive a treatment for his lungs, which seemed to help, but the big change came about when his daughter, Linda, arrived. She babied him and fussed over him, and he was eating it up! I realized that most of his issues the night before was caused by difficulty in breathing and acute loneliness. Hmm!

I dropped off to sleep somewhere in there and managed a couple hours' sleep before Robert woke up and started shouting again. I took in a breath, ready to give him a piece of my mind then stopped.

"Robert," I said softly, "Push the button. Just push the button."

My voice was still a little husky from the tube through my nose and throat earlier in the week, and the words must have seemed to come from out of the air. I mused later that he might have thought it was God's voice, without the burning bush this time, but whatever he thought, he was silent. A few seconds later, I heard the buzz of his bed controls as he pushed that button…the wrong one.

"The other button, Robert," I told him. "The one on the board."

"I can't reach it," he said after a moment. "I don't know where it is."

I heaved a sigh and knew there was only one choice. I got out of bed, pushed back the curtain separating us, and found the board with the call button. He was right. It was behind him and out of sight (only the Lord knew how it had been pushed back there). He couldn't see it. I handed it to him, indicated which button was the call button, and went back to bed.

Chronicles of A Blessed Man

The nurse, a quiet lady from somewhere in South America, came in, adjusted his position, and that problem was taken care of.

A while later, one nap later to be precise, Robert was uncomfortable again and managed to push the correct button on his own. The staff were apparently busy. For one thing, the lady I had heard howling earlier was in pain again. The poor soul. So, I finally got up, pushed the curtain aside again, and asked him what the problem was.

"My neck is bent funny," he said. "I need someone to move the pillow."

I carefully moved one of the pillows until he was more comfortable and finally went back to my own bed, feeling rather good about my attitude. I hadn't had to be gruff with the old guy after all.

A peaceful night resulted from then on. The next sound I heard was the change of shift.

Paul Haber

CHAPTER 24
LESSONS AND ESCAPES

Saturday morning with a good night's sleep! I couldn't believe it, but there it was. Robert was stirring over in his bed, but we had both managed to sleep most of the night. Part of the improvement, of course, was due to the medical procedure he had received the previous day aided by the arrival of his daughter, Linda. Robert was a lonely, lonely man.

Actually, I woke up at about four-thirty, dreaming about being knocked off a horse by a bright light. It sounded pretty familiar. I guess it was a carry-over from the previous night when discovering my own "road to Damascus." I couldn't sleep anyway, so I pulled myself out of bed, and found a Bible I had asked for a day or two earlier. (King James Version, in a Catholic Hospital. Go figure!)

Chronicles of A Blessed Man

I didn't want to turn on my bed light and possible wake Robert, so I disconnected my IV from the wall, gathered all the stuff I thought I would need, bible, glasses, pitcher of water, and a chair, and moved it all into the hallway that was lit up as always.

Either Kyehwa had brought the wrong glasses or something else was wrong because I still had trouble focusing on the small print in the Bible, but I was determined. I flipped pages until I found Acts and began to read. I had read the story of Saul's conversion many times before, but this time, it seemed a little closer—not that I consider myself in the same league as the man from Tarsus, but the connection with his life and what had just happened to me was too close for coincidence. It took an hour and a half, but I made it through the part where Saul gets blinded by the light and wanders around in darkness until a man named Ananias is told by God to go and bring Saul in.

I had to smile. I had my own Ananias, but his name was Larry Cornett, who had "brought me in from darkness" when he and his wife, the other Linda, invited Kyehwa and me to a Bible-study, two years before. I had been saved several years before, but while I had read the Bible, I had never really studied it the way we did with

Paul Haber

Larry—dissecting the meaning of every verse. I knew now that it had all been preparation for this week.

When I had made sure I understood about Paul's conversion, I went back to bed, thought about how it all applied to my life, and dropped off to sleep in just minutes.

Robert and I were served our breakfast. In my case, eggs, bacon, and pancakes, washed down with juice, milk, and coffee. No, I couldn't finish it, but oh, I tried! To help the breakfast settle, I hauled myself out of bed and took a walk, about twenty minutes' worth, then settled in to read for a while and to watch a little television.

Robert was working on some crossword puzzles Linda had brought on Friday, so I started a channel check just to see what was playing. Let's see. Cable TV in September about noon…football!

I swear it wasn't my fault. The TV just locked up on ESPN, and I couldn't get it to change to a more educational channel. Yeah, right! I can't tell you today who was playing, but it beat staring at the ceiling.

I remembered I had a roommate, so I called over, "Robert, do you like football?"

"Yeah," he replied, "I do."

"How about if we watch a little today?" I asked.

Chronicles of A Blessed Man

The enthusiasm is his voice gave me my answer. "Good idea," he replied.

If you live in Arizona, the games held in the East began about noon, and the last games on the West Coast ended about six or seven pm. To say we watched a "little" football would be an understatement. We gorged on football, we od'd on it, carrying on an interrupted dialogue during commercials or after an especially good (or bad) play. I pushed the divider screen back, so we could see each other, which seemed to make communication a little easier. The games continued through lunch. I kept watching when Robert's daughter arrived for a visit, and I think we were both about ready to quit when my visitors began to arrive.

Shamelessly eves-dropping on Robert's conversation with Linda, I gathered that he lived in a "retirement" home when he wasn't suffering from pneumonia as now. I already had learned from one of the techs that Robert served as a volunteer in this very hospital, pushing patients' wheelchairs and other tasks to make them comfortable. I had also learned that rather than being in his late seventies, as I had guessed, Robert was 92 years old. I was amazed! Despite his illness, he was in remarkable condition for a man his age. I have to admit I had figured he had been "rode hard and put away wet" and so looked older than he was rather than the opposite.

Kyehwa came and stayed for several hours. I took a short break from football to go for a walk around the ward with her, and after she left, David and Ruth Parker came.

Ruth, the ever-patient wife of a martial arts "freak," put up with our shop-talk and even managed to interject some good advice when I explained about my quandary concerning my martial arts teaching. I felt I should return to "my roots" in Okinawan/ Japanese karate, but at the same time, I did not want to insult the Dai-Shihan-Joseph Holck, who was one of the founders of the art of Kajukenbo in which I had been promoted to seventh degree black belt a couple of years prior. I highly respected Professor Holck for his accomplishments in the martial arts. He was a tenth degree in Danzanryu Jujutsu as well, and I highly appreciated the way he and his wife, Aimee, had taken me into their marital arts family even to the extent that she referred to me as "one of her boys." It didn't occur to me until days later that the situation paralleled my questions about my Christian walk.

David helped me to see that the two were not mutually exclusive. Kajukenbo was very eclectic, and I

Chronicles of A Blessed Man

could teach it in a more traditional style if I so chose. Sounded pretty simple once he explained it that way. With that problem solved, we discussed technique, philosophy, and I gave him a short report on each of the two books he had lent me a few days prior both of which I had read through once already.

It was curious that while I was talking about returning to roots, one of the books he had brought was about a sensei (teacher) named Mas Tsuroka, who had headed the very first style I had studied after returning home from the Marines in 1967. The other book explained several other terms and principles that had always troubled me. The "light went on!" All in all, my stay in the hospital had been very educational in my martial arts study, not to mention every other facet of my life.

Shortly after the Parkers left, another friend and fellow martial artist, Paul Lapointe, arrived with one of his students. I had known Paul since he was a teenager. In fact, I had been instrumental in teaching him Karate and Jujutsu at one point. We mostly discussed the latest gossip in the Kodenkan Yudanshakai, our organization, and our hopes for the future.

After Paul left, one of his students named Zach came to visit the "sick, old Shihan." I warned him not to underestimate this sick old man, especially since I was between him and the door. We both chuckled.

After an hour or so, Zach left, and I collapsed back into the pillows. It had been a long day. I glanced over toward Robert's bed and found he was sleeping. Good! I fussed around for a little while before surrendering to the fatigue and dropping off myself.

We didn't make it all the way through the night. Robert woke up several times as his neck was cocked at an uncomfortable angle or he needed a drink. I was a little surprised at how patient I was with him that night, which was quite different from the first night. I found that unless he needed to be lifted, which I wasn't ready to try, I could save everybody time and trouble by getting up and fixing whatever it was. I could straighten his pillow, put his pitcher within reach or whatever, and even helped call the nurse once when I couldn't handle the problem myself.

All-in-all, though, it was a pretty restful night. My help got Robert back to sleep much faster, so I could sleep too. At one point, I remember wondering if I would be able to drop back off or was going to remain awake for the rest of the night. I wondered if I were going home soon. It all depended on the tests I've had on

Chronicles of A Blessed Man

Friday, but none of the doctors had come in with a decision yet. Maybe on Sunday… I slept hard.

CHAPTER 25
FREE AT LAST!

Sunday at last.

I awoke with the sun in my eyes. I had left the blind open the night before, and sunlight was streaming in the window. I fumbled around and found my glasses. Seven-thirty.

Shift change had already happened, but no one had made it in to do the latest round of vitals. Since I was eating solid food, the IV only contained saline, and the flow was turned off.

Sometime during the night, the night nurse or maybe tech- I didn't even open my eyes- had asked my full name and birth date again and plugged some sort of antibiotic into the thing. Before the night shift left, they turned the flow back off. I was still attached because the tube for the IV ran all the way through my arm into my chest then into the vena cava, the large vein running into the heart.

Chronicles of A Blessed Man

I hauled myself out of bed and dragged the IV tree to the bathroom. I was getting pretty good at it by this time and did the usual morning thing—teeth, face, and comb hair. I still couldn't take a shower because of that tube to the vena cava, but I managed to get cleaned up without slopping too much water on the floor.

After drying off, I moved back into bed. As I passed Robert's bed, I noticed he was awake and alert. I greeted him and asked him how his night went. It was a rhetorical question since every time he woke up twisted in the wrong position. I ended up being the one to "fix him." It saved waiting for the staff to be summoned. Besides, it wasn't that big a deal, just moving a pillow or a blanket.

Breakfast arrived, and it was devoured and coffee savored as I turned on the television. I did a "channel check" to see if there was anything of interest on this early Sunday morning.

Hello! The TV "just happened" to be on ESPN, and the first picture I saw was a tall, long-legged woman (girl?) with dark hair wearing a pretty blue tennis dress. What a coincidence! It was the National Tennis Tournament from New Jersey someplace. Green grass, beautiful view, and the scenery was pretty impressive too.

Paul Haber

"Hey, Robert! Do you like watching pretty girls in short skirts?" I called through the divider.

"I sure do!"

"Cool! How about some tennis?"

"That sounds great," he chuckled.

Good. that settled that. For the next two or three hours, we kept ourselves busy watching people, male and female, bash a tennis ball around, a skill I have never developed. I remembered the last time I had "played" tennis many years before in Korea.

My opponent served, and I returned the serve…right over the fence! After we recovered the ball, he served again, and I returned the serve straight into the fence about head high and at about Mach 2. Needless to say, it was a very short match that day. But it has never stopped me from enjoying the young people who could do it—especially the ladies.

Somewhere along the way, doctors started coming in. I was especially glad to see Dr. Song. He was the physician who filled the slot for Primary Care for the entire hospital. He was also the guy who had nixed my release on Saturday or maybe even Friday because of a low white cell count. The surgeon and the pulmonary specialist were willing to let me go home, but Song talked them out of it. His feeling was that it was better to

Chronicles of A Blessed Man

treat any infection in the hospital rather than chance it getting worse and result in my re-admittance. I couldn't argue with that. This had led to the CAT scan on Friday just before dinner.

Song brought good news! The CAT scan showed no infections and voila! The white blood count was normal again. He couldn't explain what had happened, but neither he nor I wanted to look a gift horse in the mouth. He told me he had already spoken to the other two doctors, and they all agreed that I could go home today. Sunday. Well, okay, since the tennis was over anyway... Yippee!

I grabbed my cell phone and gave Kyehwa the good news. She could pick me up about eleven am. Now I was excited! There were a few things to accomplish though. First, a team from somewhere came, had me don a surgical mask like theirs, and after a complete round of sterilization, proceeded to remove the IV tube from my arm. They told me to blow on command. I did, and they pulled out a tube that seemed to go forever. This is when they explained where the tube actually ended, a scant distance from my heart in the Vena Cava. I was impressed and listened very carefully as they explained the procedures I needed to follow for the next few days. I knew I didn't want an infection in that vein!

Paul Haber

Once everything had calmed down, and I was no longer attached to any IV tree or anything else, I took a short walk and proceeded to get dressed. Kyehwa had brought my clothes a couple of days before, and it felt good to be wearing real clothes again.

After I dressed, and the staff had all left us alone for a while, I walked around the divider into Robert's area.

"Robert, my name is Paul, and I am your friend," I said, stealing a line from Leadership guru, John Maxwell. It was true in a way. I had done all I could to make him comfortable in the last couple of days and nights. "Would you do me a favor?"

"Of course," he answered. "I would do anything for you."

That struck home. Maybe we had become friends.

"Robert, would you please remember that you're a dignified gentleman of ninety-two years and that you can do anything?" I said softly. "The other thing I want you to remember is to find the right button and push it."

This brought a smile since "push the button" was the first thing I had ever said to him, and he remembered.

"I will," he said. "Thank you."

I went about my chores, getting everything packed and ready to "blow this pop stand" as I told the nurse. The day nurse came in and told me they would miss me.

Chronicles of A Blessed Man

They didn't get very many patients who made things as pleasant as I had. I got choked up. It was then I realized that for the last day or so, most of the staff had been using my given name instead of the usual "Mr. Haber." The only exception, of course, was when they verified my identity before administering drugs.

I felt a little humbled. Maybe this "nice-er guy" thing was a good idea. I didn't usually deliberately intimidate or aggravate people, but I had become pretty good at it over the years. It was going to take some work to change that habit, but I was determined to make it happen. Frankly, it was for my own sake as much as for others. I liked the way I felt when I added value to someone else's life.

That would be one of several lessons I would spend time thinking about in the next few days. Maybe that was the whole point of this "exercise," necessary changes.

Kyehwa arrived and hauled all the stuff I was taking home, laptop, cards, books, and all the rest. One of the techs, a Russian lady named Natasha but whom everyone (except me) called "Comrade," volunteered to escort me to the door. I didn't have to ride in a wheelchair, so I made my escape as quickly as I could. I still had some potted flowers a neighbor had sent, so as I passed the Nurse's Station, I donated them to "brighten the place" as I told the nurse.

Natasha helped me into the car and said goodbye again calling me "Paul." I was making friends faster these days.

By the time we drove back to our home in Benson, I was exhausted. I slept in my own bed for the first time in almost two weeks.

CHAPTER 26
THE NEW BEGINNING

The next several days were filled with recovery, gaining strength rapidly, and the nights were filled with cryptic dreams. Slowly, with Kyehwa's help, I began to understand all that had happened in the past two weeks.

Then, like today, I had huge gaps in my memory of the events—especially those between the onset of pain and waking up in ICU. Only later did I remember preparing to go to Marina's house to cut grass. At first, it was only a blank. Now, not then, I remember filling a small workout bag with leather gloves and a few small tools I thought I might need.

I remembered the sudden sharp pain in my belly, thinking it was caused by what I had eaten that morning, dry rice, and trying to expel it from my stomach with no result. I recall curling up into a ball on the floor of my bedroom unable even to stand erect. I vaguely remembered begging Kyehwa and Marina to take me to the Emergency Room.

From there, it's bits and pieces. I remember being in the car and realizing that we had passed the turnoff for the "short-cut" to Benson. I asked why but don't recall whether I ever got an answer. I can still see the view as we drove into the Benson Hospital, first going to the wrong door before reversing our path and going to the ER. I still don't recall getting out of the car. The next bit I can see in my memory is lying curled up on a bed or gurney with my head on some sort of table. The pain was so great that I couldn't straighten my body.

Then I woke up in ICU a week later. I'm told that my pain was misdiagnosed as a kidney stone (in the lower abdomen?) and that because of the terrible storm that day with all the accidents occurring in the downpour, it took seven hours to get an ambulance to take me to St. Joseph's Hospital in Tucson. Okay, if you say so. I don't remember.

For several days after I was released from the hospital, I sat on the sofa with Kyehwa, taking notes as she related what had happened from her view. This was interspersed with several short walks a day, starting with walking halfway up the short hill to the south and back.

Chronicles of A Blessed Man

It was less than a hundred yards, but it seemed so very difficult.

Then I would sleep and dream. Thank Heaven, these dreams weren't like the ones I had the first few days after regaining consciousness, but I dreamed of changes I needed to make in me such as the way I acted and even the way I thought. I discussed some of them with Larry Cornett, some with Kyehwa, and some with David Erickson, my mentor in business. I began a long and gradual path to the type of attitude and life I hope to solidify in the coming years.

For the past several years, I had looked after my body with proper diet and exercise, but any changes I had made mentally or spiritually just sort of happened. Now, I was, and am, making a deliberate campaign to become the "nice-er guy" as I had promised my friends while they visited in the hospital.

The strange serendipity of all this is the large number of new people who have entered my life—some before the illness, who helped bring about the changes, and others who have miraculously appeared in the interim. Even the way I teach the martial arts has been affected, more smiles and less growls. I know my students appreciate the difference.

Paul Haber

I have several goals for the next few years, all tied in with what I envision as the "three-lane highway" that I travel toward what the Almighty wants me to accomplish. I use my martial arts and fitness to get the attention of those to that approach with the answer. I use Bible study and my Christian walk to reach others. For still others, the business opportunity I have been engaged in for years is the proper approach. If I can become their friend as I help them make more money, I can also teach them, by my words as well as my actions, how to become closer to God. In a few cases, one lane leads to another and then to another. Only an All-powerful Lord could plan this. No, I do not believe in coincidence.

I realize that not everyone I meet, even some of you who are reading this, agree with my beliefs. That's okay. We each have to walk the road for ourselves. But every faith I have ever been in contact with has one thing in common. The Golden Rule. If I can do this for others, then some of them will do likewise to others. Voila! The world is improved one life at a time.

I have always known that, but I have certainly not always practiced it. Due largely to the strange sequence of events, which, I have to believe, were orchestrated and managed by God, or a Higher Power, use whichever

Chronicles of A Blessed Man

term you prefer, I now strive daily to "walk the walk" instead of merely talking it.

Perhaps, the most interesting and exciting difference in the post-emergency world is the renewed closeness with my children. Some of them dropped everything in their lives to rush to my bedside, and some were unable to. But I know in my heart that all of them worried, cared, and loved. I don't think I have always deserved that much, but I'm working on it. Thanks, kids. I love you.

I thank you who have suffered through this attempt to discover and understand myself and what happened to me and my family. I hope you've enjoyed my rambling reminiscence, and I hope you will pray to whatever Power you believe in that I can continue to change myself and whatever part of the world I can touch.

Meanwhile, I will pray that you and those around you will experience the great feeling of peace that surrounds my life now. I have always wondered what true peace was. Now, I know.

###

Paul Haber

Chronicles of A Blessed Man

Paul Haber

About the Author

Paul Haber is a former career soldier- a Marine, then Special Forces (Green Beret) and Ranger. After retiring from the service, he held several jobs, including security officer, bodyguard and martial arts instructor, before "finding his niche" with the Arizona Department of Corrections; progressing from Officer, to Sergeant, to a type of counselor called Corrections Officer III, until taking an early retirement in 2008.

His personal life was not quite as successful. Ten years after a marriage to a woman he barely knew, he became divorced and hurried into another, against the advice of his parents and friends. He didn't realize at the time that he was, in great measure, the cause of the split with his first wife.

Fortunately, his second wife, Kyehwa, would not give up on him, despite the usual- and some not so usual- problems in their marriage. Her upbringing and her beliefs were strong enough that she persevered, and slowly taught him the meaning of love, responsibility and marriage.

Shortly after retiring from Law Enforcement Paul was suddenly struck down with a ruptured small intestine, which brought him hours, possibly minutes, from a painful death.

This is the story of that time, what he learned and the beginning of a new way of life.

Made in the USA
San Bernardino, CA
05 December 2018